CW01082329

TREASURES OF THE
THUNDER DRAGON

TREASURES OF THE
THUNDER DRAGON

A PORTRAIT
OF BHUTAN

ASHI DORJI WANGMO WANGCHUCK

Queen of Bhutan

PENGUIN
VIKING

VIKING
Published by the Penguin Group
Penguin Books India Pvt. Ltd, 11 Community Centre, Panchsheel Park, New Delhi
110 017, India
Penguin Group (USA) Inc., 375 Hudson Street, New York, New York 10014, USA
Penguin Group (Canada), 90 Eglinton Avenue East, Suite 700, Toronto, Ontario, M4P
2Y3, Canada (a division of Pearson Penguin Canada Inc.)
Penguin Books Ltd, 80 Strand, London WC2R 0RL, England
Penguin Ireland, 25 St Stephen's Green, Dublin 2, Ireland (a division of Penguin
Books Ltd)
Penguin Group (Australia), 250 Camberwell Road, Camberwell, Victoria 3124, Australia
(a division of Pearson Australia Group Pty Ltd)
Penguin Group (NZ), 67 Apollo Drive, Rosedale, North Shore 0632, New Zealand
(a division of Pearson New Zealand Ltd)
Penguin Group (South Africa) (Pty) Ltd, 24 Sturdee Avenue, Rosebank, Johannesburg
2196, South Africa

Penguin Books Ltd, Registered Offices: 80 Strand, London WC2R 0RL, England

First published in Viking by Penguin Books India 2006

Text and illustrations copyright © Dorji Wangmo Wangchuk 2006

10 9 8 7 6 5

ISBN 9780670999019

Typeset in *Sabon Roman* by SÜRYA, New Delhi
Printed at Pauls Press, New Delhi

To the Most Precious Treasure of the Thunder Dragon
His Majesty Jigme Singye Wangchuck

CONTENTS

ILLUSTRATIONS

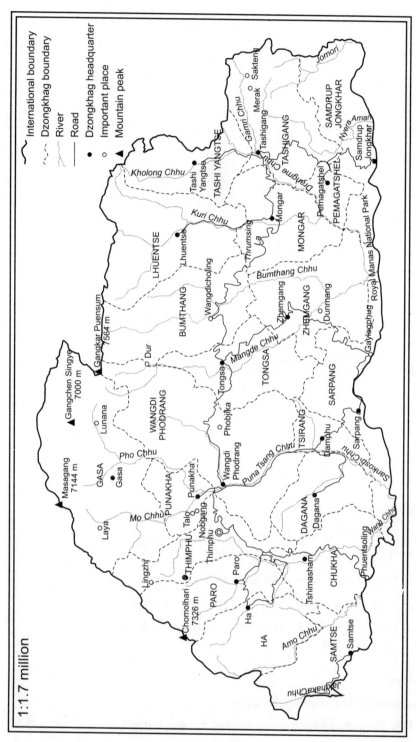

Administrative map of Bhutan

AUTHOR'S NOTE

Over the past seven years, I made several journeys on foot to different parts of my country. Often, while travelling by car, I would catch glimpses of distant valleys and villages, of temples and monasteries perched on peaks and ridges, and would long to go and explore those places. They lay along footpaths and mule tracks, which once used to be vibrant with pilgrims and monks, caravans of traders and herdsmen, and rural families on the move, making the kind of journeys I remembered well from my childhood—for that was how we all travelled in the days before the automobile came to Bhutan.

I finally decided that I must fulfil my desire to meet the people and see the places that were well off the beaten track while I was still physically fit enough to do so—because these journeys could be gruelling, involving crossing mountain passes above 5000 metres and trekking for seventeen days at a stretch through jungle-covered hills and valleys. I am grateful to Karma Ura, who helped me plan my travels on foot to different parts of Bhutan. I made detailed notes during these journeys, and it is thanks to the urging and encouragement of my editor at Penguin, Nandini Mehta, that I have written this book, a full ten years after writing my first book. Both Karma Ura and Nandini have made very helpful suggestions for correcting and improving my manuscript. My Bhutanese readers might find that in many places I have explained at some length aspects of our history and culture that they are already familiar with—I hope they will bear with me, because my publishers were insistent that I also keep in mind the reader who does not know Bhutan. Kama Wangdi and Rinchen Wangdi, two fine Bhutanese artists working at the Voluntary Artists' Studio of Thimphu (VAST), have vividly captured the unparalleled scenery of our country—from glaciers to subtropical forests—in their paintings. Their styles reflect an imaginative synthesis of the rules of classical Bhutanese iconography with more contemporary perspective-based art.

While I always prefer to travel incognito, it was not always possible to do so, and I am grateful to the district officials who on so many occasions helped make my journeys more comfortable. Though I have not mentioned them individually, I was accompanied during my journeys by a set of wonderful travelling companions. Together we experienced enthralling landscapes, breathless climbs and knee-crunching descents. But nothing was more rewarding for us than the encounters with people during these journeys, and the generosity with which they shared their lives and their homes with us. Their spirituality, serenity and fortitude, the integrity and harmony in their way of life, have taught me invaluable lessons that I try to take forward in my life. Right from my first journey, my aim was to try and help especially vulnerable people—children, the elderly and the disabled—through scholarships, medical support and monthly stipends. And thus was born the Tarayana Foundation, which supports scores of such people whom I first met on my travels. Though many of them live in the most remote parts of the country, the Tarayana Foundation provides the link that keeps us in regular contact.

Above all, it is my Beloved King who has been my inspiration, a king who spends each day in the service of his people.

17 December 2005   DORJI WANGMO WANGCHUCK

INTRODUCTION

'Bhutan? Isn't that the place they call the Last Shangri La?'
'Bhutan? Isn't it that kingdom frozen in the medieval ages?'

The outside world's reactions to Bhutan tend to swing between two extremes—it is perceived either as a paradise on earth or as a country completely isolated from the rest of the world and trapped in a time warp. Neither image is true. But it *is* true that Bhutan is like no other place in the world. Its spectacular natural beauty and pristine environment, its fabulous architecture and living spiritual culture, and its wise king whose unique philosophy of governance measures the country's progress and development not by its gross domestic product (GDP) but its gross national happiness (GNH)—this is the stuff of which legends, and romantic flights of fancy, are born.

The Land and the People

For centuries, until the building of roads in the 1960s made the country accessible, Bhutan was known as the forbidden land. Its isolation was not a deliberate political or historical choice, but more a consequence of its geography. As Captain Pemberton of the English East India Company noted in 1838: 'The whole of Bootan territory presents a succession of the most lofty and rugged mountains on the surface of the earth . . . The consequence is that the traveller appears to be shut out on every side from the rest of the world.' A later British colonial official, who seemed terror-struck at the prospect of a journey to Bhutan, wrote in 1894: 'No one wishes to explore that tangle of jungle-clad and fever-stricken hills, infested with leeches and the pipsa fly, and offering no compensating advantage to the most enterprising pioneer. Adventure looks beyond Bhutan. Science passes it by . . .'

Such misconceptions and exaggerations about Bhutan were typical until about fifty years ago, and are not uncommon even today. So perhaps it is best if I begin with some facts. Bhutan is a small country in the Eastern Himalayas, nestled between two giant neighbours, India and China. It is bordered on the north by China's Tibet Autonomous Region and on the east, south and west, respectively, by the Indian states of Arunachal Pradesh, West Bengal and Assam, and Sikkim.

Our own name for our country is Druk Yul. The legend goes that when the great Tibetan saint Tsangpa Gyare Yeshe Dorji (AD 1161–1211) was consecrating a new monastery in Tibet, he heard thunder which he believed to be the voice of a dragon (*druk*), loudly proclaiming the great truths of the Buddha's teachings. He named the monastery 'Druk', and the religious sect he founded 'Drukpa Kargyupa'. When this school of Mahayana Buddhism became Bhutan's state religion in the seventeenth century, the country was named Druk Yul, or the Land of the Thunder Dragon.

The profusion of temples and monasteries throughout the country—there are more than 2000 of them—and the ubiquitous presence of red-robed monks indicate the important role that Buddhism plays in almost every aspect of Bhutanese life. Every district in the country has a *dzong*—an enormous fortress—which houses the official monk body and several temples. And every village has a temple, around which the life of the community revolves. Hinduism, the other major religion in Bhutan, is followed by people of Nepali origin belonging to different castes such as Chhetri, Rai, Tamang and Gurung, who are collectively known as the Lhotsampas. They are settled mainly in southern Bhutan.

Bhutan's official language is Dzongkha, spoken mainly in western Bhutan, but there are two other major languages—Sharchopkha, spoken in eastern Bhutan, and Nepali, in southern Bhutan. In addition, there are as many as nineteen major dialects, which have survived in pockets, in isolated valleys and villages which are cut off from neighbouring areas by high mountain barriers.

Bhutan's area is 38,394 square kilometres—about that of Switzerland—and its population is 552,996. So the population density is low—about fourteen persons per square kilometre—and every Bhutanese owns his own land. We are still predominantly an agrarian country, with 69 per cent of the population dependent on agriculture for their livelihood. However, only 8 per cent of our land is arable. Some 72 per cent of Bhutan's territory is under forest cover, and nearly 20 per cent is under perpetual snows.

Our national dress is the *kira* for women and the *gho* for men. The kira, a rectangular piece of woven cloth about the size of a single bed sheet, is wrapped around the body, secured at the shoulders by a pair of silver clasps called *koma*, and at the waist by a tight belt called the *keyra*. An inner blouse with long sleeves called the *wonju* and an outer jacket called the *tyoko* complete the outfit. The art of weaving, which is only done by women, is highly developed in Bhutan, and an elaborate kira can take a whole year to weave. Unusually for Asian women, most Bhutanese women have short-cropped hair, cut in a fringe across the forehead, though young women in our urban centres increasingly sport long hair. The man's gho is a one-piece costume rather like a kimono with broad white cuffs, which is pulled up to knee length and fastened at the waist with a belt, forming a deep pouch across the chest. This pouch is like a vast pocket, used to carry all sorts of things—money, important papers, a wooden bowl for drinking tea, some hard cubes of dried cheese to munch as a snack and a little round box for carrying *doma* (betel nut, wrapped in a paan leaf smeared with lime paste)—chewing doma is a Bhutanese passion!

The most important events in the Bhutanese calendar are religious festivals. The major ones, which attract enormous crowds, are the *domchoe*s and *tsechu*s, held annually at big monasteries and dzongs all over the country. The dates vary, but most tsechus are held in autumn, which is a leisure period for farmers (though the famous tsechu in the Paro Valley is held in spring). The highlight of a tsechu is the religious dances that are performed by monks as well as laymen in fabulous costumes and masks, while clowns known as *atsara*s, often carrying large wooden phalluses, entertain the crowds with their slapstick routines in between the dances. Many households also hold their own private annual prayers, called *choku*, followed by a feast for the whole village. (I have written in more detail about domchoes, tsechus and chokus in Chapter 2.) Dasain, also in autumn, is the big festival of the Lhotsampas, with prayers at their temples, joyous drumming and dancing, and lavish feasts, with everyone dressed in new clothes.

Archery, or *datse*, is undoubtedly Bhutan's most popular sport, traditionally played with bamboo bows and arrows, with two small targets placed at either end of the field, 140 metres apart (in international archery the target is at a distance of a mere 50 metres). On holidays, you can usually see several archery matches in progress, and people driving by an archery ground tend to hastily roll up their car windows—unlucky passers-by have been known to be hit by stray arrows, sometimes fatally. Every village has an archery ground, and at important matches the two competing teams are supported by lively groups of women 'cheerleaders' (see also Chapter 2). These days, expensive imported bows, with pulleys to increase the speed and force of the arrows, are coveted status symbols. *Khuru*, or darts, is another favourite sport, played outdoors, with the target placed at a distance of 20 metres.

Our topography has to a large extent shaped our way of life and our history. The country has aptly been likened to a gigantic and steep staircase, which rises from the foothills, at 150 metres above sea level, to snow peaks of above 7000 metres. Within a distance of only 240 kilometres, one can pass from semi-tropical to temperate to freezing alpine areas. Bhutan can conveniently be divided horizontally into three geographic zones. The foothills of the south, which rise from the plains to an altitude of 1500 metres, have thick broadleaf evergreen forests, fertile farmland and a relatively high population density. This region also has a number of trading towns, such as Phuentsoling and Gaylegphug, which have sprung up close to the border with India. The climate is warm and humid in the lower areas, and damp and misty as one rises to the hills.

The central, temperate zone, cut off from the foothills by the high ranges of the Inner Himalayas, has a succession of valleys at altitudes ranging from 1500 metres to 3500 metres. The capital, Thimphu, and most of our major towns, dzongs and monasteries lie in this zone. The hillsides here are thickly forested with blue pine and other conifers, oak, magnolia, maple, birch and rhododendron. Willow, poplar, walnut and flowering dogwood are among the trees commonly found in the valleys, where farmers grow rice, millet, wheat, buckwheat and maize, as well as cash crops like asparagus, mushroom and potato, strawberry, apple and peach, mandarin oranges and cardamom.

Above the temperate zone, at altitudes ranging from 3500 to 5500 metres, are the subalpine and alpine highlands, ringed by the towering snow-clad peaks of the Greater Himalayas, among them Mt Chomolhari (7300 metres) and our highest peak Mt Gangkar Puensum (7541 metres). These are our sacred mountains, abodes of the deities, and most of them have never been climbed. The alpine zone boasts beautiful glacial lakes, and pastures covered with carpets of wild flowers when the snow melts—among them dwarf rhododendron, edelweiss, fritillaries, anemone, primula, delphinium and our national flower, the fabled blue poppy (*Meconopsis grandis*). In the summer months the pastures are dotted with herds of yaks, and the distinctive black tents of Bhutanese yak herders. The alpine highlands are also the home of the snow leopard, the musk deer and our curious national animal, the takin (see Chapter 11).

Bhutan's rivers, which rise in high mountains, flow southwards through the country, creating deep gorges and valleys. The river waters are our 'white gold', for Bhutan's major source of revenue is hydroelectric power, which we export to India. The waters of the

Thimphuchhu (also known as the Wangchhu) power the Chukha and Tala hydroelectric projects. Other major rivers are the Amochhu (*chhu* means river) which drains south-west Bhutan, the Phochhu and Mochhu which meet at Punakha to form the Punatsangchhu, and the Mangdechhu which flows through the central district of Tongsa, and then joins the Manas, the largest river in Bhutan. All our rivers flow into the plains of India, where they eventually join the mighty Brahmaputra.

While the Great Himalayas run from east to west, many ranges of the Inner Himalayas run from north to south through Bhutan, creating formidable barriers between the valleys in the central belt. The Pelela ranges of central Bhutan are an example, dividing the valleys of western Bhutan from those of central Bhutan. In the days before the roads were built, the route to Bhutan from the Bengal plains, through the south-west of the country, was particularly difficult, as it involved walking for about a week through the humid malarial tracts and dense forests of the foothills, facing the real risk of attacks from wild animals, and then crossing raging rivers and steep passes to reach the valleys which were the historic centres of power in western Bhutan—Thimphu, Punakha and Paro. Since the early 1960s, a highway has connected the town of Phuentsoling in south-west Bhutan, bordering the plains of Bengal, to the higher valleys of Paro and the capital, Thimphu, in western Bhutan—a distance of 184 kilometres which can be comfortably covered in six hours.

Crossing the country on foot from west to east, though it took at least two weeks and involved steep ascents and descents over the series of mountains that divide one valley from another, was somewhat easier, for there was an extensive and well-maintained network of mule tracks and bridle paths connecting all the major valleys. Today, the East–West Highway (also called the Lateral Road), which was completed in 1975, makes it possible to traverse the country comfortably within three days. I will briefly describe this journey to give you a glimpse of the landscapes, historic sites and cultural traditions you will see along this road (see map on p.182).

Driving east from Thimphu, you will cross the Dochula Pass on the crest of a ridge at 3050 metres. From here, on a clear day, you will have a spectacular view of the snow-covered peaks of the Himalayas, among them Mt Masangang (7158 metres) and our highest peak, Mt Gangkar Puensum. In spring, the *Magnolia campbelli* and rhododendron trees are in full bloom in the forests around Dochula, and the air is heady with the scent of the daphne plant, from which we make paper. Passing the magnificent group of 109 *chorten*s (stupas) at Dochula, the Druk Wangyel (or Great Victory) Chortens (which I have written about in Chapter 8), the road then descends steeply to Lobeysa, where a turn to the left would bring you to the Punakha Valley, with its great dzong on the confluence of two rivers. But if you continue on the East–West Highway, you will pass the seventeenth-century Wangdiphodrang Dzong, dramatically straddling the crest of a ridge, with the Punatsangchhu river flowing far down below. Prickly cactus covers the hillsides below the dzong, an effective, if unusual, deterrent to invaders. You would now have travelled 70 kilometres from Thimphu, a journey that takes about two and a half hours.

Past Wangdiphodrang, the road begins to climb, and after 40 kilometres there is a bifurcation, which leads to Phobjika, a wide and beautiful glacial valley, 13 kilometres off the highway, at an altitude of 3000 metres. Phobjika is the winter home of the rare black-necked crane, and the site of Gantey Gompa, one of Bhutan's most famous monasteries, established in 1613. The people of Phobjika eagerly await the arrival of the cranes each year—the birds are regarded as sacred, and the popular belief is that they circle the monastery three times when they arrive and depart from Phobjika. Back on the highway, the road ascends steeply for 14 kilometres to cross the Black Mountains at Pelela Pass, at 3300 metres. If you make this journey in early spring, you may see herds of yaks which have still not gone up to their higher summer grazing grounds. If you are lucky, you may also see the Himalayan red panda, whose favourite food is the dwarf bamboo that grows around the pass.

Past the Pelela Pass, you are in central Bhutan. The scenery and vegetation change perceptibly, with the wide plateau of Rukubji stretching out, its fertile fields golden yellow with mustard or white with potato flowers, depending on the season. The road descends to the valley floor at the Nikkarchu bridge, and enters Tongsa district, passing the village of Chendebji (27 kilometres from the pass), with its great chorten built in the Nepali style. The road now twists and turns, hugging the mountainside for 42 kilometres, with awesome views of Tongsa Dzong, the historic seat of the royal family and one of the most impressive examples of Bhutanese architecture (see Chapter 14).

Tongsa Dzong is at the junction between the East–West Highway and the road to the south, which leads to Zhemgang district and on to the border town of Gaylegphug. If you stay on the East–West Highway, another 68 kilometres, crossing the Yotola Pass at 3400 kilometres, will bring you to the Chumey Valley in Bumthang district. Bumthang is famous for its distinctive woollen weaves, known as *yathra*, and at the village of Zugney you will see fine samples of yathra hanging by the roadside to entice travellers. Especially eye-catching are the colourful blankets with intricate patterns which are wonderfully warm and rainproof. Yathra is also made into ponchos, jackets, rugs and cushion covers. The weavers, all women, can be seen at their looms beside the road.

The highway continues over the Kikila Pass to enter the next valley in Bumthang—Jakar, the district headquarters, watched over by its lovely dzong, which looks like a white bird perched on the hill. The valley floor is dominated by Wangdicholing Dzong, the summer palace of the first two kings of Bhutan (see Chapter 8). Bumthang is often called the cultural heartland of Bhutan, and it would take you at least a week to visit all the sacred temples and monasteries in and around Jakar, Chumey and the neighbouring valley of Tang. Some of Bhutan's most important pilgrimage sites are in Jakar, among them the sublime ensemble of three temples at Kurjey, Tamshing Monastery with its rare murals, and Jamba Lhakhang, which dates to the seventh century. Jakar is also renowned for its locally produced Gouda cheese and honey, first introduced through a Swiss development project—don't fail to try these delicacies.

Beyond Bumthang, the East–West Highway crosses the Thrumsingla Pass (3800 metres) with a series of dizzying ascents and descents—the faint-hearted are advised not to look down into the steep vertical drop at the edge of the road! There is a poignant memorial to the men who died building this stretch of the road.

Spectacular waterfalls line the route, which goes through forests of rhododendron and conifers, and the beautiful tragopan and monal pheasants can often be spotted in this area. The road then descends into Mongar district, one of the biggest in Bhutan in terms of its population. You are now in eastern Bhutan, and would have travelled 450 kilometres from Thimphu.

But before climbing to Mongar Dzong, a road branches off the highway and leads to Lhuentse district, about 70 kilometres away. Until this road was completed in 1980 this district in north-eastern Bhutan was only accessible through mule tracks from Bumthang, with which it has had long cultural and historic links. The landscape now displays the typical features of eastern Bhutan—narrow valleys with very little flat land, villages often perched on ridges, with terraced fields on the lower slopes. Ferns and a variety of spectacular orchids grow in profusion in the forests, while maize is the main crop you will see in the fields, together with millet—much of which is turned into the home-brewed alcohol, *ara*, that is popular in the east.

Lhuentse boasts a spectacular seventeenth-century dzong, perched high on a rocky spur above the Kurichhu river, and the district is famous for the skill of its weavers. It is also the ancestral home of the royal family—Jigme Namgyel, the father of the first king of Bhutan, was born in 1825 in a Lhuentse village called Dungkar. He left home at the age of fifteen to find his fortune, became the powerful Penlop (governor) of Tongsa, and then the de facto ruler of the country in 1870. In 1999, it took me two days of walking from Lhuentse Dzong to reach Dungkar (there is now a motor road to the village), where the two fine ancestral manor houses still stand. The superb weaving tradition of Lhuentse owes much to the patronage of the daughter of Bhutan's first king, Ashi Wangmo, who became a nun and bequeathed her priceless collection of textiles to the Jangchubling Monastery above Lhuentse Dzong where she lived for some years. Even today, the most prized textiles in Bhutan are the *kushuthara* weaves of Lhuentse with luminous, multicoloured silk patterns woven against a white background. Other renowned centres of weaving are in the south-eastern district of Pemagatshel and in Khaling in Tashigang district.

Tashigang, in the heart of eastern Bhutan, is 92 kilometres from Mongar, a three-hour journey on the highway. Its historic dzong, built high on a cliff above the confluence of two rivers, was the centre from which eastern Bhutan was governed until the early twentieth century. Today Tashigang is the major urban centre in eastern Bhutan. Bhutan's first college for undergraduate studies, Sherubtse, is located about 20 kilometres from the town, in a large and beautiful campus.

From Tashigang, it is a scenic 53-kilometre drive to Tashi Yangtse district, past the sacred rock and temple of Gom Kora (see Chapter 5), on to the great chorten of Chorten Kora, built in 1740 and modelled on the style of the Boudhnath Stupa in Nepal. Its annual tsechu attracts enormous crowds, including people from Tawang in the Indian state of Arunachal Pradesh.

By now you would probably be suffering from severe road fatigue, especially after the unending series of hairpin bends that the Lateral Road makes. (The joke goes that the longest stretch of straight road in Bhutan is the airport runway in Paro!) So this is a good place to get out of the car and off the road, and make the delightful two-hour walk from the road-head to the serene Bumdaling Valley. Like Phobjika, Bumdaling too is a winter haunt of the black-necked crane—only about 5000 of this endangered species remain in the world. The birds arrive here in late October and leave in late March for their summer home in northern China. A day's walk north of Bumdaling is the sacred Rigsum Gompa Monastery, which has the most exquisite mural that I have ever seen, depicting scenes from the life of the Buddha. Tashi Yangtse district is famous too for its beautiful lacquered wooden bowls (see Chapter 5) and its Institute for Training in Zorig Chusum, the thirteen classical arts of Bhutan. Slate carving, paper-making, iconographic painting, and intricate silver and gold work are among the arts taught here (see Chapter 8). The Tashi Yangtse district is also believed to be a favoured habitat of the elusive Yeti or Abominable Snowman (see Chapter 13). People here have wonderful tales to tell of Yeti sightings, though the creature has never been captured on camera.

From Tashi Yangtse, you have to return to Tashigang to get

back on the Lateral Road, which continues on for 180 kilometres to Samdrup Jongkhar district, in the steamy foothills of south-eastern Bhutan, on the border with the Indian state of Assam. From here, an eight-hour drive westwards through the plains of Assam and Bengal would bring you back to Bhutan's south-western gateway, Phuentsoling. The traveller, having made the journey through Bhutan along the lateral east–west road, would now have a pretty good idea of the topography of the country, and the extraordinary variety of landscapes and climates, peoples, languages and cultural traditions that it contains.

History

The journey through Bhutanese history is a more complex one. Little is known about our early history, though archaeological evidence suggests that Bhutan was inhabited as early as 2000 BC. Oral tradition indicates that at the beginning of the first millennium, the country was inhabited by semi-nomadic herdsmen who moved with their livestock from the foothills to grazing grounds in higher valleys in the summers. Like the rest of the Himalayan region, they were animists and many followed the Bon religion, which held trees, lakes and mountains to be sacred.

By the eighth century, with the advent of Buddhism in the country, our history becomes closely entwined with religious figures, and the myths and legends associated with them. In the early seventh century, the Tibetan Buddhist king Songtsen Gampo built the first temples in the country, in Paro (see Chapter 9) and Bumthang, to pin down a giant ogress who sprawled across the Himalayas and had been terrorizing the entire region. But another century passed before Buddhism actually took hold in Bhutan. In AD 747, the great Indian saint and teacher Guru Padmasambhava, who had founded the Nyingmapa sect of Buddhism in Tibet, came to Bhutan—legend says that he manifested himself riding on a flying tiger—and stayed in a meditation cave in a cliff in the Paro Valley, now the site of the famous monastery of Taktsang or Tiger's Nest (see Chapter 9). After meditating there for some time, he travelled on to the Bumthang region in central Bhutan, where the ruler Sendha Gyab (also known as Sindhu Raja), having heard of his miraculous powers, had invited him to exorcize a spirit that had made him ill. The Guru converted the spirit to the Buddhist faith, and the grateful king and his subjects followed suit. The Guru then persuaded King Sendha Gyab to make peace with his enemy, King Nowache (Big Nose), at a place called Nabji (see Chapter 14), bringing to an end years of bloody warfare.

Guru Padmasambhava—or Guru Rimpoche as he is more commonly known in Bhutan—was a historical figure, who was born in Uddiyana in the present-day Swat Valley of Pakistan, and became a renowned sage in India as well as Tibet. He visited many parts of Bhutan, performing miraculous feats and winning people over to Buddhism. During this period, many local deities became assimilated into the Bhutanese Buddhist pantheon, usually as the protecting deities of a particular village or valley. Many Bon practices, particularly those which worship nature in its various manifestations, have been integrated into the form of Mahayana Buddhism practised in Bhutan. And there are still isolated pockets in the country where the Bon religion, with its shamanistic practices, lives on.

Today, Guru Rimpoche is revered in Bhutan as the second Buddha, and there is no temple, monastery or Buddhist home in Bhutan that doesn't have an image of him. He is often shown flanked by his two consorts, the Indian princess Mendharawa and the Tibetan princess Yeshe Tshogyel. At the annual tsechus held at dzongs and monasteries, the grand finale is usually a ceremony of special homage to the Guru, when life-size images of him, representing his eight different manifestations, are brought out in a spectacular procession. In almost every valley in Bhutan, you will be shown a rock or a cave where Guru Rimpoche has left his footprint, handprint or some other sign of his visit and his benediction, on a rock or a cave. Visitors might view these with bemusement or scepticism, but not a Bhutanese—for us they are especially sacred pilgrimage sites.

The era after Guru Rimpoche's was one in which Buddhism went into eclipse in Tibet. During the reign of the heretical king Langdharma in Tibet (AD 836–42), Buddhism was banned, monasteries destroyed and monks persecuted. At this time, many people from Tibet fled the country and settled down in Bhutan, mostly in the western valleys. The eleventh and twelfth centuries saw another wave of migrations from Tibet when lamas of the various sects took refuge in Bhutan, where they found growing support especially in the western part of the country. Among them was Drukpa Kinlay (1455–1529), known as 'the Divine Madman', who remains one of the best-loved saints in Bhutan (see Chapter 5). He spread his teachings through his unorthodox and often shocking behaviour, using songs and poems, earthy jokes, and his legendary sexual prowess, to draw attention to true Buddhist spiritual values. Bhutanese culture is both deeply spiritual and robustly earthly, and the wooden phalluses that you see hanging from the eaves of many Bhutanese houses as well as the flying penises painted near front doors are a typical expression of the latter.

Much of the history of Bhutan's medieval period is lost, because many historical records were lost in a series of fires and earthquakes that destroyed our dzongs, monasteries and printing presses. But enough has survived to provide an outline of major events. For much of the medieval period, Bhutan had no single dominant figure of authority. A number of local chieftains ruled different valleys and constantly fought each other. Then in 1616 arrived a figure who was to change the course of our history. Zhabdrung Ngawang Namgyel (1594–1651), descended from a distinguished lineage of great lamas, was at the age of twelve recognized as the reincarnation of the Prince-Abbot of Ralung Monastery in Tibet, the main seat of the Drukpa Kargyupa sect. His enthronement at Ralung was, however, challenged by a powerful rival claimant, whose threats and repeated attempts to overthrow him made his position very difficult. In 1616, Ngawang Namgyel left for Bhutan, entering the country through the northern region of Laya (see Chapter 11).

Very soon, he established his spiritual as well as political authority over the country, under the title of Zhabdrung (which means 'at whose feet one submits'). Zhabdrung Ngawang Namgyel was a great spiritual, cultural and military leader, and we regard him as the founder of the Bhutanese state. He repelled a series of Tibetan invasions, established the dominant position of the Drukpa Kargyupa school, formed a state monk body which was housed in Punakha Dzong and, for the first time, unified the country. He exercised his power through the series of dzongs he built right across the country, controlled by his representatives, called Penlops. The Zhabdrung also drew up a code of laws, and created cultural and religious traditions which have helped shape Bhutan's distinct identity. For example, it was the Zhabdrung who devised our national dress, and introduced the practice of holding the annual religious festivals called domchoes at Thimpu and Punakha.

The Zhabdrung instituted a unique system of administration whereby he was the spiritual head of the country, while administrative and political affairs were handled by a secular ruler called the Desi, and monastic establishments were headed by the chief abbot called the Je Khenpo (British colonial texts often refer to the Desi and the Je Khenpo as the Deb Raja and Dharma Raja, respectively).

Perhaps the first Westerners ever to visit Bhutan came during the Zhabdrung's rule—two Portuguese Jesuits, Fathers Cacella and Cabral, who arrived in 1627, have left glowing accounts of the Zhabdrung's kindness, scholarship and tolerance: 'He received us with a demonstration of great benevolence, signifying this in the joy which he showed on receiving us . . . This king has also a great reputation as a man of letters and . . . all other great lamas reverence him.' The two priests stayed for many months with the Zhabdrung in Cheri Monastery, at the northern end of the Thimphu Valley. He allowed them to preach, was eager to learn about their faith, but drew the line at converting to Christianity himself!

In 1651 the Zhabdrung went into meditation in Punakha Dzong, and was not seen in public again. He died soon thereafter but, incredibly, his death was kept a secret for more than forty years, as it was felt that news of his passing would create instability and invite Tibetan invasions again (see Chapter 8). Desi Tenzin Rabgye (1638–96), the fourth civil ruler, was the Zhabdrung's chosen heir. He ruled for fourteen years, and was a great administrator who consolidated the Zhabdrung's legacy and completed his unfinished work (see also Chapter 7). He also instituted the system of rule by reincarnations of the Zhabdrung, who would be reborn in three forms, embodying his mind, speech and body. The mind incarnation, however, was the only one who had the right to rule. In practice what usually happened was that since the Zhabdrung's reincarnations were recognized and enthroned when they were still minors, power was often exercised in their name by others, leading to vicious intrigues and tussles for power. Two reincarnations of the Zhabdrung were born in my father's family—but that is another story, which I have told later in this book (see Chapter 1).

After the Zhabdrung and Desi Tenzin Rabgye, Bhutan once again went through a long period of turmoil and instability. Several Desis were assassinated, and in the absence of a strong central authority, wars broke out between rival Penlops and chieftains. During this period, Tibetan armies invaded Bhutan three times. Bhutan also engaged in a series of skirmishes with the British in the region known as the Duars (literally doorways) in the plains and foothills of Bengal, as the East India Company was eager to wrest this fertile area over which the Bhutanese had traditionally enjoyed control. These early skirmishes ended in an uneasy truce.

In 1774, Warren Hastings, the Governor General of Bengal, eager to explore new trade possibilities, sent a mission to Bhutan led by George Bogle. Bogle spent five months in Bhutan, and fell in love with the country and its people. Since he was one of the handful of foreigners who visited Bhutan during this period, his account is worth quoting. He noted that everyone from the ruler to a humble farmer dressed the same (this is true today as well), and that:

> The simplicity of their manners . . . and strong sense of religion preserve the Bhutanese from many vices to which more polished nations are addicted . . . They are strangers to falsehood and ingratitude. Theft and every other species of dishonesty are little known. The more I see of the Bhutanese, the more I am pleased with them. The common people are good-humoured, downright and, I think, thoroughly trusty. The statesmen have some of the art which belongs to their profession. They are the best built race of men I ever saw.

Another mission sent in 1783, led by Captain Samuel Turner, recorded its 'favourable impression of the intelligence and civilization of the inhabitants of Bootan'. The surgeon who was part of this mission declared: 'I think the knowledge and observations of these people on the diseases of their country, and their medical practice, keep pace with a refinement and state of civilization which struck me with wonder.'

But by the mid-nineteenth century, relations between Bhutan and the British again deteriorated, when they fought several battles over control of the Duars on the border with Bengal and Assam, which were the only routes in and out of Bhutan from the south. In 1864 a British mission led by Sir Ashley Eden arrived in Bhutan to resolve the border dispute. But unlike his predecessors, Eden had nothing good to say about the country. The Bhutanese, he said, were 'an idle race, indifferent to everything except fighting and killing each other'; the Bhutanese mules were 'fidgety and vicious', and the music 'monotonous and noisy'. The last straw for Eden was his meeting with the Tongsa Penlop at Punakha: 'The Penlow took a large piece of wet dough and began rubbing my face with it; he pulled my hair, and slapped me on the back . . . On my showing signs of impatience or remonstrating, he smiled and deprecated my anger, pretending that it was the familiarity of friendship . . .' Later that year, the British struck back—they annexed the Bengal Duars, but the Bhutanese army led by the Tongsa Penlop fought fiercely and ousted the British in 1865. Eventually, after long negotiations, the two countries signed the Treaty of Sinchu La, in which the Duars were ceded to the British, in return for which they paid a large annuity to Bhutan.

In these troubled times a new leader emerged in Bhutan—Jigme Namgyel (1825–82), the very Tongsa Penlop who had so enraged Sir Ashley Eden, and led Bhutanese troops to victory against the British in the Duar Wars of 1864-65. Jigme Namgyel, scion of a noble family descended from the fifteenth-century saint Pema Lingpa, was a self-made man, who had risen through his remarkable abilities to become the Tongsa Penlop. He soon gained the upper hand over rival penlops and chieftains, and became the most powerful man in the land. Peace and stability returned to Bhutan. In 1870 he became the Forty-Eighth Desi or civil ruler of Bhutan for a period of three years, but remained the main locus of power even after the appointment of his successors.

The Monarchy

Jigme Namgyel's son Ugyen Wangchuck was a worthy successor to his father. He became Penlop of both Paro and Tongsa, and further strengthened his position by defeating his rivals. The reigning Desi was by now a mere figurehead, and Ugyen Wangchuck became the unchallenged leader of the country. In 1907, Ugyen Wangchuck was unanimously elected as the first hereditary King of Bhutan by an assembly of people's representatives, high officials and important lamas. He was given the title Druk Gyalpo, and his coronation day, 17 December, is now observed as Bhutan's National Day. Ugyen Wangchuck was a much-loved king, and his was a peaceful and enlightened rule until his death in 1926.

He was succeeded by his son Jigme Wangchuck, whose reign was one of peace and prosperity, and on his death in 1952, he was succeeded by his son Jigme Dorji Wangchuck. We regard the third king as the Father of Modern Bhutan. He was a visionary, who launched Bhutan on a programme of planned development that ended its isolation. Under his rule, the first major motor road was built, which changed our lives dramatically (see Chapter 3), modern education was made available to his people for the first time and a number of technical assistance programmes in cooperation with India and other countries were started, to develop agriculture, hydroelectric power and a modern system of administration. He also instituted a National Assembly composed of representatives of the people from all parts of the country, as well as officials and members of the clergy, and set up ministries, a high court, a currency, and banking and postal systems. In 1971, Bhutan joined the United Nations. In just two decades King Jigme Dorji Wangchuck propelled Bhutan out of the medieval ages and into the twentieth century.

The third king died tragically young in 1972. His son Jigme Singye Wangchuck became the fourth Druk Gyalpo, and the youngest monarch in the world, at the age of sixteen. In 2007, Bhutan will have had a monarchy for a hundred years, more than a third of which will have been under the reign of the present king.

Modern Bhutan

The new king's coronation ceremony in 1974 focused the world's attention on Bhutan. It brought the international media to our country for the first time, and photographs and articles published in international journals projected Bhutan as a fairytale kingdom ruled by a dazzlingly handsome young king. Soon after his coronation, King Jigme Singye Wangchuck announced his philosophy for the future development of his country. He declared that Bhutan's growth and progress would be guided, as well as measured, not by its gross domestic product but by its gross national happiness. It was a revolutionary new concept, and one that initially invited much scepticism from economists and other development experts. GNH was a nice catchphrase, many of them said, but on what index do you measure happiness? Today, the success of his gross national happiness theory is widely recognized, and has become a model for economists and planners the world over.

Put very simply, GNH is based on the conviction that material wealth alone does not bring happiness, or ensure the contentment and well-being of the people; and that economic growth and 'modernization' should not be at the expense of the people's quality of life or traditional values. To achieve gross national happiness, several policy areas were given priority—equitable socio-economic development in which prosperity is shared by every region of the country and every section of society; conservation and protection of the pristine environment; the preservation and promotion of Bhutan's unique cultural heritage; and providing good, responsive governance in which the people participate. These are the principles that have driven the King's policies.

The highest priority has been given to rural development through making health care and education accessible to all, including those living in the most remote villages; the building of roads and communication; the launching of livestock and agricultural development schemes and their associated industries; and promoting traditional handicrafts—all of these aimed at improving rural livelihoods and creating new job opportunities.

Bhutan's environmental protection measures have been drawn

up keeping in mind the mistakes made by other countries in our neighbourhood. They include laws to ensure that forest cover in Bhutan never drops below 60 per cent, and that any industrial and commercial activity that causes environmental deterioration and threatens wildlife is not permitted (see also Chapter 5). This policy has, for example, resulted in all our hydroelectric projects being run-of-the-river, with none of the ecological damage and submersion of habitats caused by large dams. Stringent eco-sensitive measures have not affected the profitability of Bhutan's power projects—they now provide 40 per cent of the country's revenue, and will ensure our economic prosperity and independence. Environmental as well as cultural concerns have also dictated the decision to discourage mass tourism, and to forgo the exploitation of many of our rich natural resources, such as copper, which would result in the destruction of human as well as natural habitats.

The unique cultural traditions which give Bhutan its distinct identity are preserved through laws such as those that require all Bhutanese to wear the national costume in public (this also keeps alive our wonderful weaving tradition), and make it mandatory for all buildings, private and public, to follow the designs and rules of our superb traditional architecture (and this certainly does not rule out having every modern convenience inside). The traditional arts and crafts are encouraged, with the highest standards maintained through the regular patronage of the government and the clergy, and through large projects for the restoration and renovation of dzongs and monasteries.

Our spiritual culture permeates every aspect of our lives, including the government. The state-supported monk body, with a strength of about 5000, is headed by the Je Khenpo or chief abbot, who is elected by the central monastic body, and is the spiritual head of Bhutan (the present Je Khenpo is the seventieth in an unbroken line). Even in the twenty-first century, monks continue to play an essential role in the life of the community, presiding over festivals and rites of passage, and providing guidance, advice and solace. About another 3000 monks are supported by private patronage. We also have the institution of lay monks called *gomchens*—these are people who live with their families, yet have acquired the religious teachings that allow them to conduct prayers and other religious ceremonies. They play a particularly important role in eastern Bhutan, travelling from village to village where their services are needed. Since monks are highly educated, greatly respected in our society, and influential in shaping opinion, they now play an important new role in national life—as highly effective agents of social change in fields such as public health, family planning and AIDS awareness and prevention.

There is now concrete evidence of the achievements of the GNH policies. From 1985 to 2005, life expectancy in Bhutan went up from forty-seven years to sixty-six. Literacy has increased from 23 per cent to 54 per cent, and enrolment in primary schools has reached 89 per cent. There are now thirty hospitals in the country, 176 basic health units and 476 educational institutions. In the field of environment, Bhutan has been named as one of the ten biodiversity hotspots in the world, for the wealth of its biodiversity and the exemplary management of its natural resources. These successes are due in a large part to the King's close personal supervision of the implementation of policies—he spends a large part of his time travelling through the country, often on foot, to make his own assessment of the progress of projects and to hear what the people have to say. Every Bhutanese has access to the King, and can personally present him a petition.

The King's goal of providing responsive and participatory governance is one that he has been working at steadily for twenty-five years, introducing fundamental changes in slow and steady phases. In 1981, for example, he began the process of decentralization and democratization by giving each of the *dzongkhags* (districts) in the country the power to determine its own developmental priorities. In 1991, he extended this decision-making power to the villages. Then, in 1998, against much resistance from the National Assembly (more than two-thirds of its members are elected representatives from the twenty districts in the country), he divested himself of his executive powers and transferred these to a council of ministers. He also pushed through a law that gave the National Assembly the power to call for a vote of confidence in the King—he insisted this was a safeguard that was essential for the future well-being of the country. And in 2001, he launched the drafting of a Constitution that would give Bhutan a two-party electoral system, and a constitutional monarchy, with a mandatory retirement age of sixty-five for the monarch (the King turned fifty in November 2005). The draft constitution is now ready and has been presented to the people for their views. In late 2005 the King started touring each district of the country to hear the people's opinions, clarify their doubts, and personally explain to them how the Constitution will make them the masters of their own destiny, in a parliamentary democracy headed by a constitutional monarch. And on our National Day, 17 December 2005, he announced that he will step down as King in 2008, and be succeeded by his eldest son, Crown Prince Dasho Jigme Khesar Namgyel Wangchuck, who would be the guardian of the new Constitution. History will, I believe, judge the reign of Druk Gyalpo Jigme Singye Wangchuck as the Golden Age of Bhutan.

Bhutan does not want to keep the outside world and the twenty-first century at bay. We want prosperity, but not at the cost of our cherished traditions and culture. We want the benefits of modern technology, but at our own pace, according to our own needs, and when we feel the time is right. It was why we waited until 1983 to build an airport and start air services to Bhutan; why we gradually increased the number of foreign tourists from 200 in 1974 to 14,000 in 2005; and why we introduced television only in 1999. People often wonder for how long, in this age of information technology and an increasingly globalized economy, Bhutan can retain its distinct identity and its deeply spiritual culture. I personally don't have any doubts on this score. You only have to see how adeptly a Bhutanese monk uses the computer to prepare a scroll of 100,000 prayers to put inside a prayer wheel to realize that Bhutanese society is both vibrant and deeply rooted in tradition, that it has an extraordinary capacity to appreciate, absorb and adapt new ideas, and effortlessly make them a part of the Bhutanese way of life.

A Word about This Book

Treasures of the Thunder Dragon is not a scholarly book on Bhutan, nor does it try to be a comprehensive one. My portrait of my country is one that is drawn from a very personal perspective, and based almost entirely on my own experiences. This book is divided into three sections. The first section, 'Growing Up with Bhutan', is a personal memoir, which describes my childhood years and my schooldays. It is a portrait of life as it was in a Bhutanese village before the country opened up to the outside world, and recounts the great changes that took place in our lives as Bhutan emerged from its isolation in the early 1960s, with the building of motor roads and the access to modern education.

The second section, 'The Way We Are', attempts to explain, again largely through my own experiences, some of our most fundamental beliefs and practices, such as reincarnation, our system of traditional medicine, our architectural traditions, and the ways in which our spiritual beliefs have helped preserve our environment.

The last section, 'People and Places', is based on my extensive travels on foot to different parts of the country, mostly to places well off the beaten track. Some of these journeys were pilgrimages to sacred sites, but most were to villages, communities and remote habitats that have rarely seen outsiders, and are little known even to most Bhutanese. They resulted in heart-warming encounters with unforgettable people, they opened my eyes and my mind to the needs and problems of people who live far away from Thimphu and other centres of government, and led me to discover places of unimaginable beauty.

I hope this book will provide some new insights into Bhutanese character and culture, give some glimpses of the magical beauty and diversity of our land, and convey the pride that all Bhutanese take in being the children of the Thunder Dragon.

PART ONE

GROWING
UP WITH
BHUTAN

CHAPTER 1

THE VILLAGE ON
TREASURE HILL

I was born on 10 June 1955 as the sun's first rays touched the mountains of Nobgang, a village in western Bhutan, in the Punakha district. My father acted as the midwife, cutting my umbilical chord with a sharpened bamboo stake before handing me over to my maternal grandmother, Ugay Dem. By the time I was born, my father was an experienced hand at this task, for he had delivered my two older siblings, my sister Beda and brother Sangay, as well. There's a family story that as each of her children was born, during the worst of her labour pains, my mother would beat my father on his head, so that he too would experience a bit of the pain she was suffering, and my father would submit to this bashing with perfect good humour.

In keeping with childbirth practices in Nobgang, my father's duties at my mother's bedside would continue for several more weeks as he nursed my mother through her convalescence. For two months after each childbirth, my father would be kept busy chopping logs of wood to heat water in a gigantic cauldron in the outdoor bathhouse for my mother's twice-daily baths. The boiling water would be poured into a wooden tub and allowed to cool naturally to the right temperature, and then my father would carry my mother from the bedroom to the bathhouse, bathe her and carry her back to bed. For extra strength, the new mother was fed eggs fried in butter, and *maru*—a dish made with minced dried beef, ginger and a touch of chilli. To keep her relaxed and contented she was also served *chungkay*, a fermented rice porridge cooked with butter and eggs. No doubt my mother, with doting parents and a loving husband, was nurtured with extra tenderness, but in those days everyone in Nobgang set great store by the curative powers of warm baths, and maintained that women should rest completely for two months after each delivery, as this would ensure that they stayed strong and youthful. Modern medicine might scoff at these beliefs, but my mother, who has borne and brought up nine children, is a remarkably youthful seventy-year-old.

Nobgang village is perched high on a ridge above the Punakha Valley. It was founded by the Ninth Je Khenpo, Shacha Rinchen, who was the chief abbot of Bhutan from 1744 to 1755, one of the most revered and learned religious figures in the country. The legend goes that while he was in meditation in a remote retreat in the mountains above Nobgang, he noticed a sparkling light, like a brilliant star, in an area that was then a jungle, some distance below. He sent a monk to investigate, and the monk was astounded to see a stone radiating light. He promptly took the stone to his master who declared it was a gemstone (*Nob* in Dzongkha). And so he named the place Nobgang, literally Treasure Hill, and built a temple there called Tsolhakhang. He interred the luminous treasure inside an image of the Buddha in a chapel on the third floor of the temple.

There is a powerful legend attached to this image. In the 1950s there was an epidemic of smallpox in Nobgang and several neighbouring villages. Many people succumbed to the dreaded disease, but after the first death in Nobgang a curious thing began to happen to the statue—its outer layer began to blister and peel off, and there were no further smallpox deaths in our village. The people of Nobgang believed that the Buddha had absorbed the disease in order to spare them from the worst of its ravages. Later the image was repaired and given a new coating of gold. But to this day a small dot, like a pockmark, remains on the face of this serene Buddha. This dot moves its position every few years—earlier it was on the cheek, and now it has emerged on the upper lip. No amount of gilding can cover it up.

Some years after the Tsolhakhang temple was built, the tenth chief abbot of Bhutan built another temple facing it, the Zimchu Gomo temple. The village of Nobgang grew up around these two temples. Had I been born thirty years earlier, I would not have been born in my grandmother's house in Nobgang, but in birthing shacks located on the outskirts of the village. For in those days, strict monastic rules had to be followed by the residents of Nobgang. No animals were allowed to be kept in the village, not even birds. Only a lone rooster, who served as the community's alarm clock, had the privilege of living there. Neither weaving nor farming, the usual occupations in villages, was allowed. A monk with a fearsome leather whip ensured that the monastic rules were observed. Despite these restrictions, people were attracted to settle there because as a monastic village Nobgang and its inhabitants were exempt from the compulsory labour tax then prevalent in Bhutan. The labour tax, known as *woola*, meant that for every building project in the country, be it the construction, repair or renovation of a monastery, dzong, road or mule track, people were obliged to contribute a certain amount of their labour. The monastic rules that governed Nobgang were relaxed only in the 1930s.

There were more than fifty houses in Nobgang, strung out in a line along the ridge. Our house, situated on the highest point in the village, was a large double-storeyed one, with a walled outer courtyard and a smaller inner courtyard. It was made of rammed earth and stone, with carved wooden windows and lintels, and a broad pitched roof covered with wooden shingles, weighted down with stones. There was an open space between the top floor and the roof, which was used to store firewood and hay, and to dry chillies and meat. In those days most village houses in Bhutan used to stable their livestock on the ground floor, but we had our spacious kitchen and grain store here. There were five rooms upstairs, including bedrooms and an ornately decorated chapel. From the top floor a rectangular room jutted out at a right angle from the house, so that the shape of the structure was that of an inverted L or, as we liked to say, a flag (*tharcham*) on a mast. These tharcham houses were unique to Nobgang. From our house on the crest of the hill there were wonderful views of the snow-capped peaks to the north, and the wide and fertile valleys of Punakha and Wangdiphodrang to the east and south.

Just outside the west door of our walled courtyard was a paan leaf grove, and near it grew indigo and rubia plants, which were used to dye blue and red the yarn that every household wove into cloth. Nearby was our bathhouse, with its large wooden tub, and fig trees and wild raspberry bushes growing around it. My mother, a stickler for cleanliness, made all her children wash their clothes and bathe here in hot water every alternate day. This meant the consumption of large quantities of firewood, which we would get from the forests nearby. Pear, peach, orange and persimmon trees surrounded our wheat fields to the north of the house, while Sichuan pepper bushes and *guendrum* (*Diospyros lotus*) trees grew around a chorten nearby. Also outside our walled compound was our latrine, its wooden floor supported by eight-foot-tall poles above a pit.

Running the entire length of the village was a water channel, made of hollowed-out logs, propped up on wooden poles. The source of the fresh water which flowed through the channel was a spring above the village, shaded by a large tree entwined with gourd creepers—these were lovely to look at but not to eat. The gourds, hollowed out and dried, were used as ladles in every Nobgang house. Being the first house in the village, our house was the first to collect water from the channel. We would store it in great copper urns in our courtyard, as would households further down who would tap it at the point closest to them. If people wanted to quench their thirst, they simply had to put a leaf into the channel to divert the water towards them. This water channel was the daily meeting point in the village, where people would gather, exchange news and pass on messages. The channel came to an end at a chorten at the far end of the village, where people living in the lower half of Nobgang would collect their water. It was not only the lifeline of Nobgang, it added character to the whole village and knit it together.

While my mother's family had been settled in Nobgang for a long time, my father's family made their home here much later, after a period of considerable turmoil in their lives. This was caused by a tragic event which affected not just my father's family, but had repercussions throughout the country. To explain its significance, I need to go back a bit into history.

As I have written in the Introduction, Bhutan was unified and given its administrative structure in the seventeenth century by Zhabdrung Ngawang Namgyel. The founding father of our country, he was in his lifetime the supreme authority in Bhutan. After his death there followed a long period of dual rule—by a temporal head (the Desi) and the ecclesiastical head (the Je Khenpo). In addition, spiritual power rested in the three reincarnations of the Zhabdrung, representing his mind, speech and body. The Mind Reincarnation, in particular, was traditionally held to have the right to exercise supreme authority in Bhutan. With the introduction of monarchy in Bhutan in 1907, the system of dual rule came to an end. But the three separate reincarnations of the Zhabdrung's mind, speech and body continued to be recognized and greatly revered by the people.

In the early part of the twentieth century, two of these reincarnations were born in my father's family. My father's uncle (his mother's brother) Zhabdrung Jigme Dorji (1905–31) was the Sixth Mind Incarnation, with his seat at the great Talo Monastery, an hour's walk uphill from Nobgang. And my father's elder brother Jigme Tenzin (1919–49) was the Sixth Speech Incarnation with his seat at Sangchoekor Dzong in Paro. In his childhood, my father regularly went to stay with his maternal uncle, the Mind Incarnation, Zhabdrung Jigme Dorji, at Talo.

In November 1931, during the reign of the second king of Bhutan, Zhabdrung Jigme Dorji was assassinated at Talo Dzong, asphyxiated in the dead of night with a silk scarf stuffed down his throat. He was just twenty-six years old. My father's uncle was a deeply religious person, with no temporal ambitions, but some powerful courtiers feared that he could become a challenge to the king's power, and they poisoned the king's mind against him. In this atmosphere of intrigue and suspicion, some of the Zhabdrung's own courtiers also created mischief, challenging the king's authority in the Zhabdrung's name. The murder of Zhabdrung Jigme Dorji was covered up. His body was hastily cremated, and the news given about that he had died suddenly in his sleep. People throughout the country were stunned and grief-stricken, and whispers and speculation about his death continued for decades to come.

My father's family was, naturally, deeply shaken by this event. Moreover, they now feared for the life of my father's elder brother, the Sixth Speech Incarnation, Jigme Tenzin. They were particularly apprehensive about the powerful regional governor of western Bhutan, the Paro Penlop, who was a cousin of the king. He had allegedly played a major role in the assassination at Talo. Moreover, he bitterly resented the status my father's family enjoyed. He never missed an opportunity to harass them, and forced them to sell him their beautiful home in Paro, Kuengacholing, for a pittance. Fearing for the young boy's life, my father's family fled Paro, leaving behind their lands and property. My father was then eight years old. For the next sixteen years his family lived in self-imposed exile, and suffered tremendous hardship, moving from place to place—Tibet, the Haa Valley in Bhutan, Gangtok in Sikkim, and finally Kalimpong in India.

In 1947, the king sent word that my father's family should return to Bhutan, and that their lands would be returned to them. My father, then twenty-two, came back to Bhutan to serve the royal court at Wangdicholing in the Bumthang Valley. He also travelled to the Punakha Valley, to inquire about the restitution of the family's ancestral land in the valley, and stayed on to attend the annual domchoe at Punakha Dzong (see Chapter 2). My mother, dressed in her beautiful white kushuthara kira and a string of corals, was there too, and it was love at first sight. Their romance blossomed at the tsechu at Talo Monastery, which takes place soon after the Punakha Domchoe. My father was determined to come back and marry her. We still have the photograph he took of her at the Talo Tsechu, with the camera he had brought from Kalimpong. In 1949, my father's parents returned to Bhutan and, at my father's urging, settled down in Nobgang. They bought a house in the middle of the village, facing the Zimchu Gomo temple. Tragically, on their way back from India, my father's elder brother, the Sixth Speech Incarnation of the Zhabdrung, died of malaria in Tongsa, at the age of thirty. In 1949 my parents began their married life—he was twenty-four and my mother eighteen.

I was extremely fortunate in my childhood to be surrounded by two sets of loving grandparents, who were wonderful role models. My mother, Thuiji, was the only daughter of her mother, and so it was my father who moved into his wife's family home. My maternal grandmother, Ugay Dem, was unquestionably the boss of the house. Indeed, she was a figure of authority in the village, where she and her best friend Ugay Pem used to dictate decisions at village meetings, sitting under the old peach tree near the Zimchu Gomo temple. The tree, believed to have been planted when the temple was built in the eighteenth century, used to be covered with beautiful blossoms in spring. It was an education to see how my grandmother tackled people with a mixture of diplomacy, command, accommodation and fearlessness to get her way. She not only managed to make people accept her point of view, but to end up thinking that it was originally their own as well. The women of our village had the reputation of being strong and independent. The joke in Nobgang was that if a man were to become the husband of a Nobgang woman, he should come with his sleeves rolled up, ready to take on any task she assigned him. Grandfather Samdu Nob certainly came with his sleeves rolled up. He was my mother's stepfather—her biological father had left the family when my mother was a year old—but had brought up my mother with unstinting love. He was a tremendously hardworking man, a devoted husband and a much-loved grandfather.

Grandmother Ugay was a slim and petite woman with chiselled features, a renowned beauty in her youth. She was a superb cook, and prepared all the family meals. She was also a skilled weaver whose fine textiles earned her a considerable income. My mother also did some weaving, but her main responsibility was to look after her growing brood and tend the kitchen garden. Though Grandmother Ugay could not read or write, she had memorized prayers that took hours to recite. She was an excellent and pragmatic manager, and firmly assigned responsibility to her husband and son-in-law for all the tasks that needed to be done. There were our paddy fields down in Punakha to be tended, seasonal vegetables and grains to be planted, cattle and horses grazed, logs to be chopped. All these tasks were uncomplainingly carried out by Grandfather Samdu Nob, assisted by my father. Grandfather's strong hands were so roughened with work that without flinching he could pull up huge bunches of stinging nettles to feed the cattle. Many were the nights he sat up, guarding the crops, orchards and livestock from the depradations of bears, wild boar and leopards.

I still remember the excitement one evening when a leopard stealthily followed my father right to the wall of our house in Nobgang, and bit a gaping hole in the neck of his horse, before loping off to the house next door, where it made a meal of their cat. Another evening, my father encountered a bear near the fence of our house, attracted there by our fruit-laden pear tree. As the huge animal leapt towards him, my father shot it with the rifle he used to carry for protection against such encounters. The bear fell with a thud beneath the pear tree, and the next morning the whole village converged on our lawn to gloat over the death of the bear, which had been eating their fruit and killing their pigs. They also came to marvel at my father's marksmanship—his single shot had hit the bear inside its open mouth.

We loved and respected Grandmother Ugay Dem, but it was

Ashang Samdu Nob that we felt close to (Ashang means uncle and we called him that because our mother did). A lean man with a kindly face, it was he who taught us our prayers, and enforced discipline. He also taught us the traditional Bhutanese etiquette—how to receive guests, show respect to elders and religious figures, and conduct ourselves during prayers and visits to temples and dzongs. At mealtimes he would ensure we ate without dropping food or wasting a grain of rice. Sometimes, he would tie my left hand behind my back to ensure I ate with my right hand (I remain unreformed!). Grandfather Samdu Nob was a fount of folk wisdom, and some of his favourite proverbs are permanently impressed on my mind. Here are some of them, though they sound so much more poetic in Dzongkha:

> 'To know your limitations is the mark of a wise person.'
> 'Never perform all the thoughts in your mind; never speak all the words that come to your lips.'
> 'The way the arrow is targeted is more important than the way it is shot; the way you listen is more important than the way you talk.'
> 'It's no use burning the incense after the lama has left; it's no use drawing your sword after the bear has run away.'
> 'If you give someone a seat, he will soon ask for a place to stretch.'
> 'There is no tree without knots, and no person without faults.'
> 'Better to possess one virtue than a hundred nuggets of gold.'

Though we lived with my maternal grandparents, we spent a lot of time at my paternal grandparents' house. Ashi Dorji Om, my father's mother, in contrast to my dynamic and practical maternal grandmother, was a gentle lady of true sweetness and piety. We called her Angay. She never spoke a harsh word or had a malicious thought. With her snow-white hair and fair, translucent skin, there was a special radiance about her. She was treated with deference and respect by the whole village, especially as she was the sister of their late revered Zhabdrung who had died so tragically at Talo. My paternal grandfather, Sangay Tenzin, whom we called Jojo, was also a man of great presence—handsome and imposing with his long beard and silver hair. His laughter lit up his face, and his magnetic personality drew children as well as adults around him. I could see why women had found him irresistible in his youth. My father's elder brother, Uncle Wangchuck, lived with them, and the children of my father's sisters were there often. These cousins were our close companions, our accomplices in all the pranks we played. The food at my paternal grandparents' house, made by their cook Mindu, was always plentiful and delicious. We grandchildren had but to ask for a favourite dish and it would immediately be made for us.

You may have gathered from what I have written so far about my upbringing in Nobgang that women enjoy a position of equality with men in Bhutanese society. Women often inherit their parents' property, and their husbands often live there with them. Women are free to marry whom they choose, and to divorce and remarry without any social stigma. And household tasks, including childcare, are shared by men and women. My earliest childhood memory is of my father carrying me on his back when I was three, securely strapped to him with a *kabney*—a long woven cloth, which was knotted across his chest. Sometimes my baby sister Tshering Pem would be strapped to his back along with me. This left my father's hands free to do other chores around the house, while we were safely with him and out of harm's way. We would peep over his shoulder, watch what he was doing and eventually fall asleep nestled against his back.

As I grew older I would gather wood, fetch water, help harvest maize and vegetables, and often take the cattle out to graze. I especially loved milking cows. I was a tomboy, and felt more comfortable in my elder brother's knee-length gho than in the ankle-length *gochu* (tunic) that small girls wore. My gochus were stitched by my father, as were the long boots I wore, with cloth uppers and leather soles. He was very skilled with his hands, as most men were in those days, able to stitch clothes and make shoes for his family, repair everything from farming implements to the house roof, as well as do fine woodwork, carving altars, lintels and window frames—these last tasks, though, were saved for the winter months when there was little work in the fields. And of course, he was skilled at delivering babies (the practice of men acting as midwives still continues in remote villages in Bhutan).

My father used to be gone for long stretches of time, loading our family horses and mules with rice, chillies and *zaw* (toasted rice made by my mother and grandmother), to barter them for dried fish, salt and tea in Phari, in Tibet. He would also go once a year to Kalimpong in India, to buy cloth, sugar, soap, edible oils and betel nut. We would count the days until his return with toffees for us, and marvel at the factory-made fabric that he would bring back, to be stitched into new clothes. For the rest, we were self-sufficient. We ate what we grew; our oil for cooking as well as for lighting the house came from mustard seeds which we pressed ourselves; we made our own butter and cheese; and brewed tea from plants that grew nearby, such as the hypericum (St John's Wort), now recognized all over the world for its medicinal properties. Every household had basic knowledge of herbal remedies, and many villages had a skilled traditional healer with an encyclopedic knowledge of medicinal plants. But of course, they were not able to save lives in cases of serious illness, where surgery or antibiotics were required. We had no access to modern medicine.

At harvest time, it was the custom for all the villagers to pool their labour and work on one person's fields at a time. When the work was done, the owner of the field would host a feast for all those who had helped him, and this was always a very jolly occasion, when many romances flowered amongst the young people. It was the same system of communal labour whenever someone in the village was building a house—everyone would chip in. Many hands made light work at these times.

We created our own entertainment. Particularly popular was *lozay*—a kind of musical debate in which the women would be ranged against the men, and in which wit and clever repartee were much prized. The women usually won.

One of my most vivid childhood memories is of a gramophone record in my paternal grandparents' house. Uncle Wangchuck had brought a hand-cranked gramophone with him from Kalimpong— a great novelty in Nobgang—and a 78-rpm record of just plain laughter. This was a particular favourite with the whole village, elders as well as children. Many were the winter afternoons when people would gather at my grandparents' house and ask for that record to be played. After listening to it for some time, the laughter would become completely infectious—everyone listening would fall into paroxysms of mirth, until tears flowed down their faces. This record, which brought fun and laughter to generations of people in Nobgang, is still in perfect condition in Uncle Wangchuck's house.

CHAPTER 2

ANNUAL RITES AND FESTIVALS

The serene rhythm of life in Nobgang, dictated by the seasons, was punctuated by many religious ceremonies and festivals through the year. These events provided us spiritual fulfilment as well as entertainment, and helped strengthen the close-knit community ties in the village. They also provided opportunities for the people of Nobgang to meet people from neighbouring villages, and strike deals for the trade and barter of goods, and the buying and selling of land and livestock. And of course, the festive atmosphere at these gatherings, with all the young people dressed in their best, was very conducive to romance.

As children, the event we looked forward to with special excitement was the two-day annual religious ceremony known as choku, held in our house every year. The purpose of the choku was to offer prayers of thanksgiving for the blessings of the year past, and for the future well-being of the family. Our choku (what is called a puja in Hindi) would be presided over by the Sixty-Third Chief Abbot of Bhutan, Je Thinley Lhendup (1896–1974), who had settled down in Nobgang after his retirement. A man of enormous learning and piety, with lugubrious eyes and a big nose, he was the spiritual pillar of the village. My grandmother Ugay Dem was his most devout follower, and as an act of humble service used to bring home his laundry. I would volunteer to wash his clothes, and revered him so much that I would take a tiny sip of the soapy water in which his clothes were soaked, as though it were holy saffron water from the vase in our chapel! The retired abbot came frequently to our house to spend a few nights, and to enjoy the delicious food prepared by my grandmother, who was famous for her culinary skills. Once, while spending the night in our chapel, he had a dream which prophesied the coming of great success and merit to our family.

Our annual choku was always held in the eleventh lunar month, which fell either in November or in December. Three monks would come to our house two days in advance to make the ritual *tormas*—these are offerings made of rice flour or wheat dough mixed with butter, coloured and sculpted into intricate and beautiful forms. The tormas would be dedicated to Chenrezig, the Bodhisattva of Compassion (Avalokiteswara in Sanskrit), Tseringma, the Goddess of Long Life and Prosperity, and the all-powerful Protecting Deities of Bhutan, Yeshe Gompo and Palden Lhamo (Mahakala and Mahakali in Sanskrit). The tormas would be placed on the altar, which always had seven bowls of fresh water on it. These seven bowls, to be found on the altar of every Buddhist household in Bhutan, symbolize the seven offerings of food, drink, water, flowers, incense, light and perfume, which must be offered to the deities every day. The monks would then lay out special ritual food offerings, and prepare hundreds of little brass lamps with melted butter and cotton wicks, to be lit during the prayers. Thangkas (large paintings framed in brocade, representing major deities or great saints) in glowing colours would cover the walls of the chapel, and silk ribbons and tassels arranged in criss-cross patterns would be hung gaily over the altar.

The abbot would arrive a day before the choku to spend the night in our chapel. We would wait for him in front of our house, burning branches of juniper—the fragrant juniper smoke being a traditional way of showing respectful welcome. At three the next morning the rituals would commence. The abbot would prostrate three times before the altar and then take his seat on his throne, while nine monks would sit in rows on the floor on either side of the altar. The abbot would have a low carved table in front of him, with the objects necessary for conducting the prayers placed on it— a *dorji* or double thunderbolt symbol, which symbolizes the purity and wisdom that brings enlightenment; a *phurpa* or ritual dagger used for purification and for subduing demonic spirits; a *damru* or double-sided drum; and a bell. The sound and rhythm of the bell and damru, together with the sonorous notes of the conch shell being blown and the clanging of cymbals, would punctuate the chanting of prayers, and create an atmosphere that was almost hypnotic. We would sit in front of the altar for hours without being aware of how the time had gone. The entire family would gather at Nobgang for the choku, which invoked the blessings and protection of the deities for the family. Salty buttered tea (*suja*), sweet saffron rice (*deysi*) and rice porridge would be served during the breaks in the prayers.

On the second and final day of the choku, we would invite the entire village of Nobgang, and our more distant kinsmen, who would stay for the whole day. Lunch and dinner would be served outside on the lawn to all of them except the abbot, who would be served on a tray in the chapel. Food was an important part of the choku, for it was a celebration of bountiful harvest and prosperity as well. Through the year, supplies of special delicacies would be saved up and put away for the occasion. There would be sausages stuffed with rice, ginger, Sichuan pepper and pig's blood; succulent pork spare ribs; crisply fried eggs; cucumber salad seasoned with ginger and fresh cheese (*hogay*); and a national favourite—*ema datsi* or green chillies cooked with cheese. Vegetables from our fields— radish, turnip, squash, mustard greens, eggplant and spring onion— would be prepared with marrow bones to give them a special flavour. My own favourite was a stew of meaty bones seasoned with chilli seeds and a bit of cheese—my grandmother's speciality. The pork would have generous chunks of fat, and all the dishes would be swimming in oil—it was regarded as stingy to serve food in which fat was added with a sparing hand.

After the feasting there would be singing and dancing, with all the village women taking part. My mother would be centre stage, for she had the most beautiful singing voice in all of Nobgang. My grandmother and my father would be filled with pride as they watched my mother perform. Before the choku concluded, the whole family would troop back into the chapel to receive blessings. Other families in Nobgang too would hold annual chokus, and we in turn looked forward to participating in their rituals and festivities.

A festival on a much grander scale was the annual domchoe at Punakha Dzong, which would attract people from all the villages in the district, even from as far away as Laya. A day ahead, our mother would lay out our clothes and jewellery—exquisite silk kiras that had taken months to weave, strings of huge corals, turquoise and *zee*s (etched agates) that were family heirlooms—and we would have a dress rehearsal, while my grandmother inspected us carefully. 'You have to look your best,' she would say. 'You may meet your future husband at the domchoe.' Indeed, this was something of a tradition in our family—my paternal grandparents had first seen each other at the Punakha Domchoe, and so had my parents.

Early the next morning we would set off for Punakha Dzong, a two-hour walk downhill. Our horses would be laden with delicacies for our picnic, as well as for the monks, for my devout grandmother Ugay Dem had many friends amongst them. In large bamboo baskets lined with banana leaves, Grandmother Ugay would pack red rice, slices of dried pork, beef cooked with chillies and radish, juicy cucumbers and a snack of toasted rice mixed with butter and sugar. There would be wooden containers filled with buttermilk and *singcha*—a refreshing, mildly alcoholic drink brewed from wheat. On arrival at Punakha Dzong, we would go immediately to the spot reserved for us by monk friends of the family. The entire area around the dzong would be thronged by spectators, and everyone would keenly eye the jewellery and clothes worn by others.

The Punakha Domchoe, which takes place in the first month of the lunar year (usually February), is a dramatic event, combining powerful religious rites with a dazzling display of horsemanship and swordplay. After the prayers and rituals invoking the protection of the deities, a historic battle is re-enacted, between Bhutanese forces and an invading Tibetan army. When Zhabdrung Ngawang Namgyel came to Bhutan from his monastic seat in Tibet in 1616, he brought with him the most sacred relic of the Bodhisattva of Compassion, known as the Rangjung Kharsapani, and interred it in a special chapel in Punakha Dzong. A huge Tibetan army marched into Punakha in 1639 to retrieve this relic but, thanks to a series of elaborate ruses, they were routed by the Zhabdrung's much smaller force. First, Tibetan spies watching from a distance saw an apparently endless stream of well-armed Bhutanese soldiers marching out of the dzong—they were unaware that it was the same small group of men who would march out of the dzong, circle it and re-enter from a hidden back door, only to re-emerge from the front door again. This made them think the Zhabdrung's army was much larger than it actually was, and that they would be hopelessly outnumbered. The second ruse worked equally well—one night the Tibetans spied a solemn procession going down to the river. Bringing up the rear of the procession was the Zhabdrung himself, carrying a casket which he threw into the river. The watching Tibetans were convinced that the precious relic had been thrown into the river. The Tibetan army turned tail and fled, believing the sacred relic was irretrievably lost. The sacred Rangjung Kharsapani relic, of course, was still safely in its casket in Punakha Dzong, where it remains (see Chapter 8).

These episodes are re-enacted every year at the Punakha Domchoe, with great pageantry and dramatic flair. Heralded by a troupe of musicians playing horns, oboes and drums, men dressed as the Zhabdrung's *pazaps* (warriors), in splendid and colourful medieval battledress, thunder in and out of the dzong, brandishing their swords to blood-curdling war cries of '*Tai ai-he-he*', while cavalrymen gallop up and down the bridge leading to the dzong. At the conclusion of the domchoe is the *Serda*—a majestic procession of monks led by the Je Khenpo (the chief abbot of Bhutan) carrying a casket, and dressed in sumptuous ceremonial robes and hats, wends its way down to the river, where they immerse a casket and some oranges into the water in a symbolic re-enactment of the victory over the Tibetans—the oranges are then triumphantly retrieved as sacred mementoes by some of the more intrepid spectators.

Year after year, the grand spectacle of the Punakha Domchoe never failed to enthral us (as it continues to do today), but the most memorable one was in 1969. One of the pazaps marching out of the dzong tripped over his long sword and rolled down the steep flight of steps at the main entrance of the dzong, landing in a bloody heap at the bottom, where we were standing. The Crown Prince of Bhutan, who was sitting at the window above the main entrance, leaned out to get a better view of the accident. And my sisters and I, at our vantage point just below the window, got a clear view of our Crown Prince. It was the first time we had ever seen him. He was breathtakingly handsome. We could never have imagined then that grandmother's prophecy would be fulfilled ten years later!

The annual tsechu at Talo Monastery, which takes place soon after the Punakha Domchoe, is a smaller, more intimate affair, and though an important religious event it is also an occasion for much fun and laughter. The entire village of Nobgang would set off for Talo with a feeling of happy anticipation, each family carrying a substantial picnic lunch. Talo was a beautiful one-hour walk uphill from Nobgang, the path winding through shady oak and pine forest. Wild strawberry and raspberry plants grew along our route, and prayer flags fluttered high on the slopes around Talo.

Talo enjoys a magical hilltop setting with magnificent views. The imposing dzong-like monastery is perched on a large flat area with wide green lawns around it, framed by towering cypresses. The temples inside the monastery are full of treasures. I quote from the description of a British visitor, Sir John Claude White, the British Political Officer in Sikkim, who visited Talo in 1905. He could just as well have been writing about Talo today:

> While at Poonakha I paid a visit to the Ta-lo Monastery which was only reached after three hours' hard climbing.

This monastic colony is a charming collection of small, well-built, two-storeyed houses, with carved and painted verandas scattered all over the hillside, each in its little garden of flowers and trees, with here and there a chapel or decorated chorten or shrine, to break the monotony.

The great temple, with its somber background of cypress and pine, dominates the scene, but higher up the beautifully decorated retreat of the late Dharma Raja formed a fitting crown to the whole group of buildings. In the great temple were many chapels, all scrupulously clean and well ventilated . . .

The principal objects of interest were two large silver chortens containing the ashes of two of the Shabdrung Rimpoches. They were highly chased and jewelled, the stones being mostly turquoise. The ceremonial instruments used by the late Dharma Raja were preserved here and were fine examples of the best Bhutanese metal work.

The carving on the pillars and canopies was excellent . . . An elephant's tusk before one of the altars measured eight-and-a-half feet, and there was a magnificent collection of embroidered and appliqué banners; in fact, the whole building was full of treasures.

On arrival at Talo, we would head for the place reserved for the villagers of Nobgang, on a slope above the west lawn of the monastery. We would sit in the shade of the pine trees to watch the religious dances that are an integral part of a tsechu—the spectacular Zhanag or Black Hat Dance which purifies the ground, drives away evil spirits and enacts the assassination of the anti-Buddhist king Langdharma; the dramatic Dance of the Drummers of Dramitse performed by twelve men wearing animal masks which celebrates the victory of religion; the sublime Guru Tshengye or Dance of Guru Rimpoche's Eight Manifestations; and many others. In between the dances and prayers we would enjoy the delightful antics of the atsaras—men in clown's costumes who would have everyone in paroxysms of laughter with their jokes, slapstick routines and mimicry, which spared no one, not even the high lamas. The atsaras provided a welcome counterpoint to the long and solemn prayers and rituals, and kept the crowd, especially the children, from getting restive. At the end of the tsechu, the great *thongdrel* or silken banner, with Zhabdrung Ngawang Namgyel as its central figure, would be unfurled to cover the entire west wall of Talo. We would pray before the thongdrel and receive its blessings before returning to Nobgang.

But the fun would continue for another few days. Immediately after the tsechu would be the annual archery match between the villagers of Nobgang and Talo, an occasion for much good-humoured yet serious rivalry. The villagers considered victory in this match an augury of good luck in the year ahead, and defeat as inauspicious. Nobgang and Talo hosted one match each, and if both teams won a match each, then the third and deciding match would be held in either village, by mutual agreement of the archers. Each side would have a supporting group of women dancers and singers, whose aim was to distract the archers of the opposing team by singing songs that lampooned or taunted them, or simply made them laugh. My father was an excellent marksman, and we all enjoyed the display of skill, the suspense, and the teasing and jokes that made up the ambience of an archery match.

I vividly remember a match in 1961, when I was six years old. I closed my eyes and willed my father's arrow to hit the bullseye of the target, 140 metres distant. This was the deciding shot, and my father won the day for Nobgang. He was draped in silks, crowned with the helmet of a victorious warrior, lifted on to a white horse and taken in regal procession around the archery grounds.

CHAPTER 3

HORSEBACK JOURNEYS

In early 1962, my younger sister Tshering Pem and I began our formal education, in the newly opened school on the lawns of the Zimchu Gomo temple. The school was a shack made of bamboo matting with a leaking tarpaulin roof. During the monsoons, the rain poured into the single classroom, drenching us as we sat laboriously writing the alphabet on our slates. Rather more impressive than the school was our schoolmaster, a handsome man who affected a British accent when he spoke English, as he had been educated at a boarding school in British India. He kept a wooden stick on his table, which he used freely to thwack unruly or inattentive students. I took good care to be neither.

My carefree childhood days in Nobgang were coming to an end. In 1963, my father decided that it was time Tshering Pem and I were sent to school in the Indian town of Kalimpong, close to the India–Bhutan border. He had already sent my elder sister Beda and brother Sangay there in 1961. My grandparents found it very hard to part with us, but my father persuaded them that an English-medium education was essential for the future of all his children. The preparations for our departure took no time—there was little to pack; we would buy whatever we needed in Kalimpong. It was a fine day in early spring when we set off. I still remember with a pang the sight of Grandmother Ugay Dem, forlornly standing on the lawn of our house and waving to us until we were out of sight. It was comforting to know that at least Grandfather Samdu Nob would be with us a bit longer—he would accompany us on the first leg of the journey up to the capital, Thimphu.

The horseback journey to Thimphu, along a well-defined mule track, took nearly three days. It took us through pine forests to the village of Laptsakha below Talo, then over the sheer cliffs at Keekri Ja—a steep and treacherous descent which had seen many travellers and horses fall to their deaths, down to the river below. From Keekri Ja we continued on to Chandana, a hallowed spot where an arrow shot from Tibet by the Divine Madman Drukpa Kinlay in the fifteenth century had landed on the staircase of a house. We stopped here for a while, to rest and to see part of the staircase which had been carefully preserved in the shrine room of a house in nearby Toebesa. Drukpa Kinlay's arrow itself, my father told us, had been interred inside a Buddha image in Tango Monastery in the Thimphu Valley.

Every time we came to a particularly narrow stretch of the track or had to cross a bridge, Tshering Pem and I would be taken off the horses and guided safely across by grandfather or father. Nevertheless, we had a narrow escape on the first day of our journey. On what seemed a safe stretch through a forest, Tshering and I were put on one horse, and tied securely to the saddle to ensure we didn't fall off. Suddenly the horse saw the black stump of a burnt tree, took fright and started galloping wildly off the path. The saddle slid under the horse's belly, with the two of us strapped to it. We hung upside down in absolute terror, and were badly cut and bleeding as the horse ran through thorny bushes. With a superhuman effort and a lot of luck, my father managed to catch and control the horse before we came to more serious harm. We walked the rest of the way, until we reached the camping ground of Lumitsawa, where we spent the first night, sleeping in the open around a campfire.

We were on the road again early next morning before the sun came up. Grandfather Samdu had ingenious ways of keeping our spirits up during the long day's march. He would hide cucumbers and oranges in the bushes ahead, for us to discover just when we began fretting with tiredness and thirst. From a strip of bamboo he would deftly fashion a *kongta*—a tiny, flat mouth instrument—that gave us hours of amusement. He also cut bamboo stems into flutes and cheerfully endured our jarring, discordant melodies.

The last stretch of the second day's journey was the climb to Dochula Pass. This stretch was spectacularly lovely, the forest ablaze with scarlet and pink rhododendrons and creamy white magnolia, and fragrant with the heady scent of daphne. The forest floor too was covered with spring flowers—iris, anemone and euphorbia—while swathes of lavender-coloured primula and deep-purple iris lined the sides of the path. After the previous day's mishap, my father and grandfather walked alongside us constantly, holding the horses' reins, and keeping us entertained with legends and folklore about the angels, demons and spirits that were said to inhabit these forests. We would be on the lookout for the prettiest flowers, which we would pick to offer at the next wayside chorten. Grandfather would caution us never to offer the lavender-coloured primulas—they were deemed inauspicious because they grew during a lean period in the year when people didn't have enough to eat. We also learnt from him why the paper on which our scriptures are written is made from the bark of the daphne plant—not only is it durable, but no worms or termites ever eat it.

By the time we reached our campsite at Yusepang, in the midst of a forest of blue pine, we were thoroughly saddle-weary. But the aroma of the delicious hot dinner being prepared on the campfire—a stew of pork and radish, accompanied by rice and grandmother's inimitable *ezay* (a relish made of red chilli paste)—quickly revived us. It was always a magical hour around the campfire at the end of a day's riding and walking during these horseback journeys—everyone would relax, tell stories, sing and laugh over silly jokes, as we sat under a sky studded with a million stars.

The next morning, the third day of our journey, we rode past the imposing Simtokha Dzong, the very first dzong built by Zhabdrung Ngawang Namgyel in Bhutan, in 1629. My father told us to take off our hats in reverence to this holy site, which covers an entire hill, following the natural contours of the ridge. Thimphu was not far now, he told us. We rode through streams, past paddy fields and a big temple on a hill surrounded by thick forest, which father told us was called Changangkha. By afternoon, we reached a large, rather marshy field called Changlimithang, with a few shacks near a chorten, and a large dzong a short distance away. This was Thimphu in 1963. From Changlimithang, where we spent the night, we would continue on our journey to Kalimpong the next day, in a motor vehicle. My sister and I, like most people in Bhutan, had never seen a motor vehicle before. In fact, we had never seen anything moving on wheels before—carts, carriages, bicycles and the like being unsuited to our rough, mountainous terrain. For journeys, everyone in Bhutan relied on horses, mules or their own feet.

The motor road to Thimphu, on which we were to travel, had been built with Indian assistance as part of Bhutan's first five-year development plan. Construction of the road started simultaneously from Thimphu and from Phuentsoling, the foothills town on the border with the Indian state of West Bengal. The first motor vehicle for passenger use, a Willys Jeep manufactured in India, arrived in Thimphu even before the road was complete. It was driven up from the plains to the point up to which the road from Phuentsoling had been completed. Then it was dismantled and transported bit by bit over steep passes and narrow trails, and reassembled again at the point where the road from Thimphu had been completed. The Thimphu–Phuentsoling road was a remarkable feat of engineering. It covered a distance of 184 kilometres, rising sharply from 150 metres to an altitude of 2350 metres over a series of sharp hairpin bends. Before 1961, the journey from the Bengal plains to the Bhutan highlands took at least a week of hard trekking. My father and others in Nobgang who had made this journey would often recount its perils—the thick fog that always cloaked Chukha, the snakes, leeches and mosquitoes that infested the dense forest, the constant fear of attacks by bears, leopards and herds of wild elephants, who would trample and uproot anything in their way, including the bamboo shelters erected by travellers. By 1963, this road was operational though very narrow in places, and still perilously prone to rockfalls and landslides.

When the first Willys Jeep arrived in Thimphu, it created a sensation. Older residents of Thimphu love to tell stories about people's first reactions to it. Some thought, when they first saw it in motion, its headlights blazing and engine roaring, that it was a fire-breathing dragon that would devour them all. Others brought it cattle feed, since this strange beast had to carry such heavy loads and cover such long distances. And then there is the story told about Bhutan's venerable Home Minister Lyonpo Tamji Jagar, a bluff, down-to-earth man—he cautioned the driver of the jeep to use only the first gear until it wore out, before using the second and third gears.

My own first reaction on seeing the jeep was sheer terror—at its size, its noise and the nauseating smell of petrol. It was with great reluctance that I climbed in, crammed at the back with my sister and some cousins for the journey to Kalimpong. My father gave us orange peels to smell, to ward off the nausea. I fought my terror all those interminable hours down to Phuentsoling, for I was sure the jeep would roll off the road and down the mountainside, or we would be crushed by falling rocks. There were landslides all along the way—we would then get down from the jeep, scramble across the fallen boulders and trans-ship to another jeep on the other side of the landslide. It was late at night when we reached Phuentsoling, where we camped near a paddy field. This is now the centre of the town, the spot where the Druk Hotel stands.

As an introduction to motor travel, it had been a kind of baptism by fire, a nightmare journey, in contrast to the three happy and leisurely days we had spent travelling from Nobgang to Thimphu. But the 184-kilometre drive on the motor road to Phuentsoling had also been like a journey to a new planet, introducing us to a world we knew nothing about. Looking back, I see that journey as a turning point in our lives—it transported us from the medieval world of Nobgang straight into the twentieth century.

We were among the early batches of Bhutanese children who went to India for their education. By the late 1950s, increasingly convinced of the need for educated manpower, the government of Bhutan began to urge people to send their children to study at boarding schools in India, where they would receive a modern education and learn English. Government officials were dispatched to different corners of the country, to look for bright boys and girls of a suitable age, and they offered generous scholarships as an incentive to parents to part with their children. In the beginning, the Bhutanese elite used all their influence to ensure their children stayed at home and were spared the rigours of what then seemed an alarming journey into the unknown. Therefore, paradoxically, it was the children of ordinary folk—farmers and villagers—who were the first beneficiaries of this educational revolution. As far as my family was concerned, they took the initiative themselves and got admission for us into excellent boarding schools in India—my father was always a man who saw far ahead of his times.

From Phuentsoling, Tshering Pem, my cousins and I had another day's journey ahead to Kalimpong. My first impression of Kalimpong was of the noise and crowds, with radios blaring, vendors shouting out their wares, horns hooting—a veritable assault on the ears of one brought up in Nobgang, where the only loud sounds we heard were temple bells, the chanting of prayers and the crowing of roosters! In the space of a few days we had been through a bewildering range of new experiences—motor cars, electric lights and, best of all, the cinema with its magical moving images!

We were lodged in Aunty Agatha's Hostel and attended day school at St Philomena's, while we waited for admission to a better school—St Helen's in the little hamlet of Kurseong, near Darjeeling. Neither Tshering Pem nor I spoke any English, but we soon picked up a smattering of Nepali at St Philomena's. My strongest memory of Aunty Agatha's Hostel is of being constantly hungry. Our elder sister Beda, by then a boarder at St Joseph's Convent, took it upon her eleven-year-old self to feed her hungry little sisters. She would buy *aloo dum* (potato curry) and puris on credit from a roadside vendor, an old woman called Boju, and then spend a lot of time and energy dodging her when she couldn't pay back in time. Our elder brother Sangay was in a school called Dr Graham's Homes, about five kilometres from our hostel. He too was often hungry, and Beda would bring food to him on holidays.

Five months after arriving in Kalimpong, we were admitted to St Helen's Convent, established in the nineteenth century by the nuns of the order of the Daughters of the Cross. My entry into St Helen's was, quite literally, a dramatic one. We were ushered in on arrival into the refectory, where the freshly swabbed floors were wet, and the chairs placed upside down on the dining table. I was wearing a new floral print dress, of which I was very proud, and I tried to look nonchalant and confident as I walked across this large hall. I skidded on the wet cement floor and landed with a thud on my backside—an inauspicious omen at the start of something new, as we Bhutanese believe. As it happened, I did not complete my high school education at St Helen's.

Life at St Helen's was a huge change from Nobgang, but we adjusted quickly, as children do. And compared to Aunty Agatha's, the living conditions were almost luxurious. Tshering Pem and I were put in what was called the Baby Dormitory. We still didn't speak a word of English. And how we yearned for our parents, grandparents and our home in Nobgang! Fortunately, the highly regulated life at St Helen's left us little time to brood. The school was an attractive double-storeyed building with gables. The three dormitories—Baby, Junior and Senior—were in a long row on the second floor, with airy verandas on either side. Each student had a bed, and a locker with a washbasin on top of it; each dormitory used different coloured bedcovers. At the end of the dormitories was a long line of cubicles with bathtubs—we had to bathe twice a week. At the side of the bathrooms were stairs leading to the attic, which was said to be haunted. While I was there, there were 180 students boarding at St Helen's. The nuns, who were American, Irish and German, were firm but caring, and I still remember them clearly—Sister Xavier, the principal; Sister Eileen Lucy, who was in charge of the infirmary; Sister Ivana, who was in charge of the refectory; and Sister Damien, who looked after the orphanage above our school.

In the dining hall, the girls were divided into three groups—'Vegetarians', 'Beef' and 'Mutton'. The Bhutanese girls were in the 'Beef' group—unfortunately, because the unappetizing beef stew in its black, murky broth was hard to stomach. We were not allowed to waste food, being constantly reminded of the 'starving millions', and I would smuggle the stew out of the refectory in my napkin and throw it away. To this day, I cannot bring myself to have beef stew. Teatime, on the other hand, was something I looked forward to—I loved bread and we could have as many slices of bread and butter as we wanted. They tasted particularly good with the pickles that we would buy in town, and effectively kept our hunger pangs at bay.

The students of St Helen's were divided into four houses, each with its own colour—St Helen (yellow), St George (red), St David (blue) and St Patrick (green)—and the four houses competed fiercely for prizes in sports and academics. As a member of the St Patrick's team, I was not very successful in sports, but I did my bit for my house by winning prizes for English literature, history and geography. In fact, I enjoyed the studies at St Helen's. There was a girl called Devika who always topped the class, but Keya and I always vied for the second position. In the lower classes we all had to study Bengali and Nepali, and later I learned Hindi as a second language. I now regret that there was no Dzongkha teacher—the presence of more than a dozen Bhutanese students in the school would certainly have justified having one. My favourite teacher was Miss Y. Fernandes. She and her sister, Miss H. Fernandes, wore pencil-heel shoes in different colours and the prettiest frocks. I looked forward to seeing them at assembly each morning, always so beautifully dressed and freshly perfumed.

I was also an enthusiastic participant in school plays, though to my disappointment I was always given male roles. I once played the Mayor of London, with a white beard and cloak, and another time

I was a farmer in a dhoti. Tshering Pem, on the other hand, always got glamorous female lead roles, and sang soprano in the school choir. Among us nine siblings, only my sisters Beda, Tshering Pem and Sonam, and my brother Ugyen have inherited our mother's beautiful voice.

A film would be screened in the school every week. I was in Class Two, in 1965, when I first saw an Elvis Presley movie. It was love at first sight, and I remain a fan. When I saw him live at Madison Square Gardens in New York in 1972, it was the fulfilment of a dream. On his death in 1977 I went to the Memorial Chorten in Thimphu, dressed in black, and lit butter lamps in deep mourning for his departed soul. We were also sometimes allowed to go to the movie hall in town. One of the films that most impressed me was *Aradhana*, starring Rajesh Khanna and Sharmila Tagore. Many scenes in this film, as also in *Mere Sapno Ki Rani*, in which the toy train chugs slowly up the winding tracks from Siliguri to the hills, were shot nearby, in Darjeeling. Of course this made us identify even more closely with the stars and I tried to emulate the way they spoke and dressed. A favourite role model was Zeenat Aman, whom I found absolutely gorgeous, and the epitome of stylish elegance.

Another source of excitement in the cloistered world of St Helen's was the sight of boys from two schools nearby—Goethals and Dow Hill. We spent much of our leisure time sitting on benches on a flat ground called the Bread and Butter Flat (because it was near the refectory and kitchens). From here there was a great view of the boys' schools. During the annual school fete and 'socials', the 'goats' from Goethals would come to meet the 'hens' of St Helen's, and there would be much excited speculation about which 'goat' fancied which 'hen'. Though we could dance with the boys during the 'socials', the nuns were strict and vigilant chaperones. I don't know if any fledgling romances between 'goats' and 'hens' ended in marriage.

Every Sunday we would be allowed to buy food from the school tuck shop. My father had left Rs 80 each for my sister and me for the nine months of each year that we were in school. We took Rs 5 every Sunday, and it was more than enough to buy a slab of Cadbury's orange chocolate, a packet of Gems, a bar of Five Star and a bag of hot, roasted *channa* (gram). Sundays also meant a compulsory visit to church for Mass—the Catholic nuns at St Helen's insisted on this, as they did on our saying grace before meals and a prayer of thanksgiving after (it was hard, though, to give thanks for that disgusting beef stew!). We soon learned the routine of Catholic church rituals perfectly, and years later, when visiting the Basilica of Bom Jesus in Goa, I found myself genuflecting before the tomb of St Francis Xavier and saying the appropriate prayers, much to the surprise of the priest showing me around.

While I went cheerfully enough to Sunday Mass, an annual ritual I absolutely dreaded was the visit to the local graveyard on All Souls' Day. The nuns would take us there at twilight to light candles for the dead. The atmosphere in the graveyard was eerie, and I couldn't help thinking of the decomposing bodies lying six feet under. How much more respectful of the dead, I thought, was our own custom of cremation. Fairly soon after All Souls' Day, on the last day of term in November 1970, I had what is called a supernatural experience. All the girls had left for the winter holidays except the students from Calcutta and Bhutan. As I got up in the middle of the night to go to the toilet, I saw near the stairs leading to the 'haunted' attic a faceless figure in a black habit and a strange-looking peaked wimple. I shrieked in terror, and ran back to the dormitory, knocking over the empty lockers in my haste. Hearing the commotion, the nun in charge of the dormitory came to see what was amiss. When I described what I had seen, she looked taken aback and said quietly that the nuns had stopped wearing the peaked wimple several years earlier. Then she made us all kneel down and pray. In Bhutan, we would have made some offerings of food and drink to appease the restless spirit of this long-dead nun.

Another unpleasant memory of school is Inoculation Day. Year after year, I would hide in the bathroom near the Bread and Butter Flat, but would eventually be found and dragged off to Dr Kumar in the infirmary. The smell of disinfectant mixed with the smell of the vaccines would make me feel violently ill, and my stomach would be knotted up with fear. Dr Kumar, a kind elderly man, would patiently cajole me to keep still for the few seconds that he needed to administer the vaccine. My phobia for injections has never gone away.

My favourite spot at St Helen's was the Grotto of Our Lady, surrounded by a lovingly tended garden full of sweet peas, geraniums, snapdragons, daisies and rose bushes. I often went there, for the comfort of seeing the serene face of the Madonna, and to get her blessings before exams, or before the long journey back home to Nobgang for the winter holidays. We would count the days to the winter holidays in happy anticipation. The Bhutan government had set up an office in Kalimpong to look after the welfare of all their students at various boarding schools in the Darjeeling district, and we would set off in a merry group, piling into jeeps for the journey to Thimphu. Here, Grandfather Samdu would be waiting with mountains of delicious home-cooked food, to take us on horseback, along the familiar, well-loved trails through forests, mountain passes and cliffs, home to Nobgang.

By 1969, a motor road connecting Thimphu to Punakha was ready, and now the journey became much easier—we only had to do the last three hours of the journey, from Punakha to Nobgang, on foot or horseback. We would arrive home just in time for the festivities of the choku, the annual prayers in our house, for which the whole family would gather. My sisters and I added exotic new items to the repertoire of songs and dances performed at the choku, as we dressed in Indian clothes and performed numbers that we had learned from Bollywood films, as well as English songs we had learned at school, to the enthusiastic approval of Nobgang's populace. The holidays would speed by all too quickly, as we attended the chokus and celebrations of other households in Nobgang, renewing friendships and our sense of belonging to this close-knit community.

During the years when we were away at school, there had been changes in my parents' life, which mirrored the changes and developments taking place throughout the 1960s in Bhutan. To augment the family income, and to secure the family's future, my adventurous father had opened a shop in the Changlimithang grounds in Thimphu, one of the first to do so in the new capital. He would sell textiles, garments, toiletries, tobacco and kitchen utensils to the rapidly growing population of the town, and supply rations to the Bhutan army as well. Then, when the government began to promote agricultural development in the first five-year plan, he bought a piece of land at Hongso, about 18 kilometres from Thimphu, and planted an apple orchard there—here too he was a pioneer. In 1968, he bought an Indian Mahindra jeep, which greatly facilitated his business, ferried his large family around, and was plied as a taxi as well. The construction boom at this time in Thimphu gave my father the idea of opening a sawmill in Thimphu, and later another one in Phuentsoling, which is still running. In all these ventures he typically saw far ahead of his times.

When the holidays ended, it was always hard to go back to the regimented world of St Helen's and to say goodbye to our grandparents in Nobgang, with whom we always spent the larger part of the holidays. At the end of the holidays in 1969, just as we were about to leave Thimphu for Kalimpong, we received news that Grandfather Samdu Nob had suddenly died in Nobgang, from a heart attack. Our cowherd Nima had found him collapsed at the hearth. Two days after his death, a parcel of food that he had sent for us arrived—it reminded us how much we had been in his thoughts till the end.

Back at St Helen's I began to feel increasingly restless. I would watch the goldfish in their pond near the nuns' parlour, going round and round in their tiny pool of water, and I began to feel the same sense of being hemmed in, in the sheltered, constricted world of St Helen's. In 1970, after eight years at St Helen's, I left, and came back to Phuentsoling, where my parents now spent the winter months, looking after their sawmill. I quickly learned to drive my father's car, practising at the helipad next to the sawmill. Within a month I drove the car up to Kalimpong, to see my younger sisters, taking my mother and elder sister Beda with me. I don't know who was the braver, my passengers or me, for the winding road to Kalimpong and the notoriously reckless drivers of Darjeeling district made this a challenging journey even for experienced drivers. But being able to drive, to feel I could take off in the car to explore distant places, gave me that feeling of freedom that I had been yearning for at St Helen's. The boundaries of my world now expanded, and limitless horizons beckoned. My world in the 1970s had suddenly become light years removed from the world in which my mother had grown up, and in which I had spent my early childhood in Nobgang.

CHAPTER 4

A HOUSE IS CONSECRATED

Over the years, my younger siblings too left Nobgang to go to school in India. Though the family home in which we had grown up still stood, none of us went back to live there permanently again. With Grandfather Samdu Nob's death in 1969, a vital bond with Nobgang had been severed, and four years later my paternal grandfather, Jojo, also passed away.

By the mid-seventies, circumstances—and destiny—had brought our family to settle down in the capital, Thimphu, where my father had built a large house, Namgaychholing, above the Jigme Dorji Hospital. In 1979, the King chose to marry my three younger sisters and me, in a quiet and very private ceremony. This was in keeping with the Bhutanese tradition, in which weddings are strictly family affairs and not marked by any public celebrations. Perhaps our marriage was the fulfilment of a historic destiny—one that united the families of the King and the late spiritual ruler of Bhutan, Zhabdrung Jigme Dorji. It was certainly the fulfilment of a prayer composed by my father's paternal grandfather, which was recited every year at our family choku. Dedicated to the Goddess of Long

Life, Tseringma, the prayer asked her to grant his wish that kings would be born from his descendants.

A public wedding ceremony was held only nine years later—in October 1988—in response to the growing public demand for celebrations in which the entire nation could participate. The ceremony took place at Punakha Dzong, the place where we had first set eyes on the King ten years earlier, and was presided over by the Chief Abbot of Bhutan and our most revered spiritual teacher, Khentse Rimpoche. By then, eight of our ten children had been born, and they all attended the wedding, looking rather bemused! Three days of celebration followed all over the country, with dances, games and feasts, to which every Bhutanese was invited.

Before the formal wedding the King took a courageous decision to set right a historic wrong. After the tragic assassination of Zhabdrung Jigme Dorji at Talo in 1931, no king of Bhutan had ever set foot there. In 1986, the King decided that the time had come for him to break this taboo—his children were the descendants of the murdered Zhabdrung, and he would go to Talo and venture to make peace with its powerful Protecting Deity, known as Talo Gyep. There was much consternation at this move among the monk body and the ministers, who feared the consequences of breaking the taboo.

I too was full of trepidation as we prepared for this momentous journey. The Talo Protecting Deity's mount was an elephant, and we had had a pair of magnificent metal elephants made, encrusted with precious stones. These were sent to Talo a day ahead of our visit, as a gift from the King. That afternoon I had a dream of a tall man in a suit and hat standing by my headboard and smiling, and at night I had another dream—this time, it was a handsome monk standing on top of the hill leading from Nobgang to Talo, and beckoning me to follow him. From my childhood I had heard stories that the Talo Gyep sometimes appeared in the guise of a man in a suit and hat, and sometimes as a monk. I took my dreams as good omens for our visit to Talo the following day.

In the mid-1980s there was no motor road to Talo, so the next morning the King, the children, my sisters and I, as well as my parents, began walking up the old footpath, which we had trod so often in our childhood. It was raining heavily, and our horses kept slipping in the wet red clay. Among the gifts the horses were carrying up for the Talo Gyep was a pair of perfect and gigantic elephant tusks—it took five men pushing and pulling to keep each horse and its precious cargo upright on the slippery path. We must have presented quite a sight—a long line of humans and horses, thoroughly drenched and struggling their way up the slope! As Talo Monastery came into view, the sun came out, and the rain turned into a light drizzle, which we regard as an auspicious 'rain of flowers'.

On arrival at Talo Monastery, the King went straight into the inner sanctum of the Talo Gyep, and spent an hour there, while the rest of us waited in the antechamber. (Protecting deities have their own inner sanctum, known as the *gonkhang*, in most temples and monasteries. The deity is often a martial figure, and his gonkhang is hung with armour, shields and weapons. Women are not allowed to enter the gonkhang—a rare restriction against women in Bhutan.)

Every protecting deity has a number that is considered auspicious—the Talo Gyep's number is eight. It is customary to throw dice in his temple, and the number one gets is an indication of good luck or misfortune ahead. When the King threw the dice at Talo, he came up with the best possible number. We took it as a sign that, finally, peace had been made between the King of Bhutan and the 'King of Talo', and a rupture that had lasted for more than fifty years was healed at last. A splendid 27-inch gold-plated statue of Zhabdrung Jigme Dorji, commissioned by the King, was later carried in a grand procession from Thimphu to Talo, with crowds of people lining the entire route to pay homage to the image. A sad chapter in Bhutanese history, and in the history of my own family, had finally been brought to a happy close.

The Nobgang house had now stood empty for some years, and in 1997 my parents decided to give it to their eldest child, my sister Beda. She decided to renovate it extensively, with the intention of spending more time there. In 1999, the renovated house was ready, and we all went to Nobgang for the house consecration ceremony. In 1997, a dirt motor road had been completed all the way up to Nobgang. The journey from Nobgang to Thimphu, which used to take three days in my childhood, now took just three hours, in a four-wheel-drive car. As my parents and I left Thimphu in the comfort of a Landcruiser, we were overcome by nostalgic memories. Changlimithang, the marshy field where we had camped in 1963, on our way to school, had become, by the 1990s, the centre of a bustling town. Changangkha Monastery, on its hill overlooking the Thimphu Valley, was no longer surrounded by thick forest; the rice fields below it were gone, replaced by streets crowded with traffic, shopping centres, hotels, apartment buildings, houses, offices and even a golf course.

My parents' lives too had seen many changes since the early sixties. From being a farmer, mule trader and cattle merchant in Nobgang, my father had successively become a shopkeeper, orchard owner and timber dealer in Thimphu and Phuentsoling; building contractor and hotel owner in Punakha; and construction agent with branch offices in different parts of the country. The trajectory of his life reflected the many new opportunities that had opened up in Bhutan over the past thirty years. It was hard to imagine that we had grown up in a world without cars and motor roads, electricity, telephones, banks, postal services or currency notes.

The Landcruiser effortlessly crossed the Dochula Pass and whizzed past our old camping grounds at Yusepang and Lumitsawa, the steep cliffs of Keekri Ja, and Talo Monastery, perched high above the road. From Darshing Gang (Flag Hill) my sister's house came into sight. It looked beautifully festive, with coloured cloth hangings strung up all around its eaves in preparation for the next day's ceremonies.

A large wooden welcome arch had been erected, festooned with flowers, leading to the area where cars would be parked, behind the house. This was where our wheat field used to be. A tall prayer flag fluttered in the evening breeze on the west lawn of the house, marking the place where our beloved grandfather Ashang Samdu Nob had been cremated. Three white tents embellished with colourful appliqué patterns had been pitched on the lawn, for all the guests who were expected the next day. The outdoor latrine was gone, but the fig trees around it looked flourishing.

The spacious ground-floor kitchen, from where Grandmother Ugay Dem ruled the roost, was now quite unrecognizable. Gone was the wood-fired earthen stove with its five openings—now there was a gas stove, a refrigerator and electric rice cookers. For electricity, brought on pylons across the mountains, had also come to Nobgang in 1997. But the dinner that Beda served us that night revived the links with the past—she had inherited my mother's and grandmother's special recipes and their culinary skills. No doubt about it, this household still served the best food in Nobgang! The walled courtyard where I used to wash clothes, scrubbing them with ash and soapnut seeds, was unchanged, but nobody washed clothes there any more—there was a big new washing machine in the house. My parents' storeroom had been converted into a plush bathroom, with running hot water, a bathtub, and a toilet with a flush.

Upstairs, a whole new floor had been added. A marble staircase had replaced the old steep wooden one. My parents' old bedroom on the second floor had been expanded by removing the wall between two rooms. It now boasted a king-size bed, which I was to share with them that night, as the house was overflowing with relatives and friends from Thimphu.

The three of us retired to the bedroom early that night. This house had so many associations for all of us, and I was not sure how I felt about all the changes Beda had made. My mother has always been a practical person; she does not dwell too much on the past and lives each day with renewed curiosity and energy. She now declared she was delighted with Beda's transformation of the house; she had made it so comfortable that we would all come back to Nobgang more often, with our children, to spend time there. My mother was right, of course—Beda had brought the house alive again and with it, our links with Nobgang.

As darkness fell I looked out of the window to see the village bathed in the golden light of a hundred electric bulbs, while down in the inky darkness of the valley below, Shelgna and Wangdiphodrang twinkled like a thousand stars. My parents drifted off to sleep. My father's mobile phone, being charged on his bedside table, was like a totem, a symbol of how even an isolated little hamlet like Nobgang was now connected to the big wide world.

Nobgang now has a community school, with sixty students and three teachers. It has a basic health unit which provides primary medical care to the villagers, antenatal check-ups to pregnant women, and a nurse who is also a trained midwife to deliver babies. There is an agricultural and livestock extension office, which helps the farmers procure new types of seeds, improve livestock breeds and adopt new farming techniques. The average income of a family in Nobgang is now around Nu 50,000 a year, earned through the sale of vegetables, fruits, surplus rice and grain. A bus comes once a week to take such farm produce to Kuruthang township in Punakha.

Only one person owns a car in the village and people still walk a lot. Even the sixty-one-year-old head of Talo *gewog* (county), who belongs to Nobgang, frequently walks between the district headquarters in Punakha and Talo, managing the steep climb in just three hours. Since the motor road was built in 1997, people no longer buy or breed horses—only one horse, retired from service, can be seen loitering about the village.

We had a field below the footpath leading down to Punakha Dzong, where our pigsty was. Though technically outside the village, it was just a few minutes' walk from the centre of the village. As the time for our annual choku prayers approached, our family would slaughter a pig to feed the guests, just as other Nobgang families did for their annual chokus. The pig slaughter was something I dreaded right through my childhood. I would run to the forest and hide there, my ears covered to block out the sound of the pigs squealing as they were bludgeoned to death. How grateful I am to Je Thinley

Lhendup, the saintly chief abbot who settled in Nobgang after his retirement, for banning this practice in the late 1960s.

Only nine tharcham houses remain in Nobgang, with their distinctive projecting balconies that give the house the silhouette of a flag on a mast. This was a delightful architectural feature quite unique to Nobgang. The other tharcham houses have now been remodelled in the more modern, box-like style, though they still have the traditional carved wooden lintels and window frames. The grey shingle roofs weighted down with round stones have mostly been replaced with corrugated iron sheets—certainly more practical and durable, if not as pretty. The beautiful old wooden water channel which ran the entire length of the village is, alas, gone, replaced by piped water which comes through taps.

The two temples—the Tsolhakhang and the Zimchu Gomo lhakhang—remain the centre of Nobgang. Both have been beautifully renovated. The gilded Buddha image in the Tsolhakhang, with the miraculous pockmark on its face, seems to have acquired an aura of even greater serenity and benediction. The main image in the Zimchu Gomo lhakhang is an exquisite one of Tseringma, the Goddess of Long Life, who rides a snow lion. She is surrounded by her four sisters, each riding their own animal—a horse, a dragon, a deer and a tiger. Our family have always been particular devotees of Goddess Tseringma. The people of Nobgang believe that any girl from the village who pays sincere obeisance to her at the Zimchu Gomo temple will find an excellent husband. My sisters and I, daughters of Nobgang and devotees of Tseringma, have absolutely nothing to complain about on this score!

The sonorous chanting of prayers from our altar room woke me at three in the morning. Beda's house consecration ceremony had begun. The altar room had been beautifully decorated with tormas, thangkas and hundreds of butter lamps. After the service and rituals in the altar room, it was time for the family and the monks to circumambulate the house, praying for the well-being and good luck of the householders. All the people of Nobgang village were there; indeed, they had been there from the day before, helping my sister prepare the feast, set up the tents, decorate the house and look after the guests.

As the women began their dances and songs, with my mother's beautiful voice leading the singing, it was as though the years had rolled back to the sixties. So many familiar faces from my childhood were there—people who still make their living from the land, readily lend a helping hand to their neighbours, celebrate their annual chokus with undiminished enthusiasm, and keep the traditional songs and rituals alive. They have been quick to adopt—and adapt to—the comforts and convenience that modern technology has brought them, yet they have lost none of their capacity to enjoy the simple, pastoral pleasures of village life, or to take on its challenges.

It is thanks to them, and others like them in rural hamlets scattered all over the country, that Bhutan's distinctive culture, with its deep respect for the spiritual life, its close communion with nature and all its elements, and its strong ties of family and community, survives and thrives.

PART TWO

THE
WAY WE
ARE

CHAPTER 5

SACRED LANDSCAPES

On the walls of the temple in my village, Nobgang, are two enchanting murals, versions of which can be seen in just about every monastery, temple and dzong in Bhutan, and many private houses as well. One depicts the fable of The Four Friends, and the other a theme known as The Six Longevities.

The Four Friends shows an elephant, a monkey, a hare and a bird, perched acrobat-fashion one on top of the other, standing under a tall tree laden with fruit. The fable relates how the elephant, though strong and mighty, needs the agile monkey to help him reach the fruit on the tree. But, it continues, there would be no tree if the bird hadn't eaten a seed to begin with and then deposited it on the soil in its droppings; and the seed would not have grown into a tree had the hare not protected and nurtured its roots underground. The elephant, the monkey, the hare and the bird also symbolize, respectively, the four terrestrial habitats—the ground, the air, the underground and the sky. The fable underlines the virtue of cooperation, and the connections and interdependence between all creatures great and small, and all the elements, in nature's cycle.

The Six Longevities depicts an idyllic landscape—a tranquil old man sits under a tree full of luscious fruit, surrounded by deer and a pair of black-necked cranes, while a stream of clear water flows through a magnificent rock, giving sustenance and life to all the plants and creatures. Its message: the secret of long life and peace is to live in close communion and harmony with nature and all its creations.

Bhutan, with its pristine environment, is something of an anomaly in South Asia. Other countries in our neighbourhood have seen their forests depleted, their rivers contaminated, their plant and animal species die out, their mountainsides scarred with quarrying and mining, and their air polluted. In Bhutan, in contrast, the forest cover has actually increased—it now covers 72 per cent of the country's territory. Rare and globally endangered species such as the tiger, the snow leopard, the rhinoceros, the red panda, the black-necked crane, the rufous-necked hornbill and the monal pheasant have found here a protected and hospitable habitat, where they thrive. And the pure air and the crystal-clear river waters are among the first things about Bhutan that strike visitors flying in from places in the region such as Delhi, Kathmandu, Dhaka and Bangkok.

Named as one of the world's ten biodiversity hotspots, Bhutan is home to 200 species of mammals and 770 species of birds (they include seventy-two of the most threatened species in the world). Over 5000 species of plants flourish in the country, including nearly fifty varieties of rhododendrons, dozens of varieties of wild orchids and such exquisite blooms as the fabled blue poppy. So why has natural conservation been such a success story in Bhutan when it has failed in neighbouring countries, despite all their laws and regulations to protect the environment? I believe the answer lies in the spiritual and religious values on which Bhutanese culture is based, which have shaped the nature of our relationship with our environment. They have had a strong influence, too, on Bhutan's developmental plans and priorities. As I have explained in the Introduction, economic and industrial development and commercial activity have never been allowed to take place at the expense of the environment. As much as 26 per cent of Bhutan's territory has been designated as national parks and protected areas, to preserve the country's biodiversity, even though some of these areas contain valuable mineral and metal deposits.

Buddhism's respect for all sentient beings, deeply ingrained in our beliefs and practices, acts as a powerful deterrent against killing animals for sport or food. The only circumstances in which it is allowed is in self-defence (as when my father killed the bear in our garden in Nobgang) or in the harsh environment of the highlands where yak-herding communities live, where male yaks are periodically culled as there is simply not enough food for the sustenance of yaks who have grown too old to be used as draught or pack animals. The taboo on killing animals in any other circumstances has, admittedly, given rise to problems—the proliferation of stray dogs in our urban centres, for example, or the destruction of crops and fruit orchards by wild boars and bears, which causes so much distress to farmers. These are moral dilemmas which we are yet to resolve.

Respect, indeed reverence, for trees is also deep-rooted in our psyche. Every Bhutanese knows that the four main events in the life of the Buddha took place under a tree—his birth at Lumbini, his enlightenment at Bodh Gaya, his first sermon in a forest at Sarnath, and his death in Kushinagar. Our village, Nobgang, had a forest behind it, and communal rules and practices ensured that trees were not wantonly cut. If someone needed wood for constructing a house, for example, the village would take a collective decision on how much wood he needed, and he was only allowed to cut that many trees and no more. New saplings were immediately planted to replace them. There were clear rules about what we could or could not take from the forest—we were allowed to graze animals, collect leaf litter and fodder, edible ferns and mushrooms, medicinal plants and herbs, dry twigs and branches for firewood—and to take no more than we needed, for Buddhism also teaches restraint. Everyone knew, too, that the trees growing around our water source were never, ever, to be cut.

A unique aspect of Buddhism in Bhutan is that it has absorbed many practices from the earlier Bon religion with its strong animist beliefs, which imbue not just trees and forests, but also mountains, rivers, lakes, rocks, caves and other natural formations with divinity.

The non-Bhutanese reader might dismiss my descriptions of deities of lakes and mountains, or of rocks and caves where saints, angels and demons have left their imprint—and these descriptions are scattered throughout this book—as flights of fantasy. But to the Bhutanese, these sacred landscapes are very real. We believe that to disturb or pollute these habitats is to invite divine retribution in the form of illness, bad luck, floods or bad harvests. Since transgression affects not just the individual but the whole community, peer pressure acts as an added instrument for enforcing these rules.

And so it is a combination of our religious beliefs, social values and customs, and the collective folk wisdom of a predominantly agrarian society such as ours, that helps to curb ecologically harmful practices, and makes the relationship between the Bhutanese and their natural environment so close and harmonious. A keen appreciation of wild, natural beauty is a typically Bhutanese trait, and few things give a Bhutanese family more joy than to visit a scenic spot that is also associated with a saint or a deity—it is a marvellous combination of a jolly picnic and a holy pilgrimage—and on holidays they will trek for hours to reach such sites. I describe below four such sacred landscapes that are particular favourites of mine.

The large and mysterious lake called Hokotsho, a five-hour trek from Punakha, is the abode of a much-revered local deity, Tshomem— or the Lady of the Lake. Framed by forests on one side, and by meadows dotted with wild flowers on the other, Hokotsho is a place of haunting beauty. We spent a memorable family weekend here recently, to celebrate the King's birthday.

Hokotsho is relatively easy to reach from Punakha. The trekking trail begins at Sirigang, a half-hour journey by car from Punakha Dzong, following the Mochhu river upstream. For the first two hours, the trail winds steeply upwards until one reaches the monastery of Chorten Nyerbo, where stands an ancient sacred oak tree. I recommend breaking journey for an hour or so at this magical spot. According to legend, the area around Chorten Nyerbo was once a dense forest where evil spirits dwelt. One day the revered fifteenth-century saint Drukpa Kinlay, the Divine Madman, arrived here when all the demons were gathered together in conclave. He hurled a blazing log into the gathering and all the evil spirits were scorched to death. The great oak tree is said to have grown out of the blazing log that Drukpa Kinlay threw and, intriguingly, its bark is still a dark, burnt brown. This tree is much venerated by people who live in the villages around and, following their example, I too broke off a bit of the bark to keep with me as a good-luck talisman.

Drukpa Kinlay's descendants made their winter home in this area, while their summer home was at the great fortress monastery of Tango in the Thimphu Valley. The mule track connecting Chorten Nyerbo and Tango is still in good repair and frequent use, and makes a wonderfully scenic trek from Thimphu, via the Sinchula Pass. (I have done this trek in one long day—it took thirteen hours of not-too-strenuous walking, but I would recommend a more leisurely pace, with a night spent camping en route to enjoy the beauty of the forests and the wild flowers.) The monastery of Chorten Nyerbo, built in the eighteenth century, is a little-known treasure, with its magnificent statue of Maitreya (the future Buddha) and fine images of the great lamas of the Drukpa lineage.

From Chorten Nyerbo, the path to Hokotsho Lake is a gradual climb through a landscape that has remained unchanged over the centuries—handsome old village houses made of rammed earth and timber, well-tended paddy fields and meadows dotted with grazing cows, giving way to dense forests of oak and magnolia. The lake comes into view suddenly, round a bend in the trail, and takes one's breath away—an enormous expanse of deep green, reflecting the hues of the forest. Hokotsho, at an altitude of 2000 metres, is a large lake by Bhutanese standards—it takes a whole day to walk around its circumference. With its thickly wooded banks, its many little coves and bays, and the legends of the Tshomem who lives in its inscrutable depths, there is an aura of romance and mystery about this lake. Villagers from the nearby hamlet of Kabjesa told us tales of people who had disappeared and then reappeared weeks later, after they had appeased the Tshomem with prayers and gifts. Her underwater retinue is believed to include lovely mermaids and a fierce black bull who sometimes emerges to inseminate the cows of Kabjesa.

Careful to begin our visit on the right note, we reverently poured fresh milk into the lake as our offering to the Tshomem, before we settled down to enjoy a picnic on the banks. In the afternoon light, the lake surface took on a golden topaz hue, prayer flags fluttered from poles planted between rocks, and reeds swayed at the water's edge. Partridge rustled in bushes, eight ducks glided by and fish jumped in the water, watched by a trio of eagles. We could see the distant snow-capped peaks of Lunana, in Bhutan's northern highlands, against a clear sky—and I thought how different was the beauty of this lake from the glacial lakes of Lunana, set like bright jewels in their stark landscape. As night fell, and the birds flew home to nest, Hokotsho looked like dark crushed velvet spangled with silvery moonlight. Nothing had changed at Hokotsho, observed the King, who had last come here as a schoolboy thirty years earlier, except that the lake now had more fish and birdlife.

There was a brief period, however, when human encroachment threatened this lake's serene and immaculate surroundings. Some years ago, Hokotsho began to attract large crowds who would gather on its shores for an annual three-day religious festival. They would come with intricately sculpted tormas (butter sculptures), bells and cymbals, and the sound of their prayers and chants would echo across the waters. In the evenings they would light *karmi*s (earthen lamps), which they would place on little wooden planks and float on the lake, so that its surface looked like a thousand flickering flames. Beautiful and stirring though this religious festival was, the then chief abbot of Bhutan (the Sixty-Seventh Je Khenpo) took a typically wise and far-sighted decision. He declared that these large congregations, with all their accompanying noise and litter, were defiling the sanctity of Hokotsho Lake and its deity. He put a stop to the festival. Now this sacred abode of the Lady of the Lake looks like virgin territory once again. May it remain so forever.

Not quite as easy of access as Hokotsho is the Rangtse Ney in Samtse district in southern Bhutan. This is an enormous cave, which can accommodate a thousand people, and is perhaps the most extraordinary natural formation I have seen. Hundreds of caves in Bhutan have acquired a special sanctity because saints and holy men have meditated in them, and because of these associations the areas around them are like mini-sanctuaries, jealously protected by the communities that live in their vicinity. The Rangtse Ney is one of the most revered of such sites because of its association with Guru Padmasambhava. My opportunity to go to Rangtse came in 2003, when I went on a walking tour of Samtse district, to meet people who lived in some of Samtse's most remote villages.

Starting from the little town of Chengmari, the first day's walk took me to the villages Lamjee and Gowchu—a gruellingly steep climb, during which one of our best horses, carrying our food supplies, slipped off the path and fell a hundred metres to his death. I could only be thankful that he wasn't carrying a rider. The silver lining on this gloomy day was the opportunity it gave me to get to know my remarkable travelling companions—Gup (county headman) Gautam Subba and his wife, Meena Thapa, who administers this area—a real 'power couple'! The redoubtable Meena, mother of three young children, sported five earrings in each ear and wore her hair in a jaunty ponytail—she and her husband kept us informed and entertained throughout the trek.

After spending the night at Gowchu, I climbed the snow-covered Deorali Pass the next morning, and by late afternoon we were at the Sherpa village of Yoekha which, it seems, had already started festivities before I arrived—they were none too steady on their feet as they performed their welcome dance! In less than an hour from Yoekha we were at Rangtse village, with its twenty-seven households, where I spent the night. As is usual on my visits to remote areas, I spent the evening talking to the villagers about their special problems and needs, while the doctor accompanying our group attended to those who needed medical care. I spotted a seventy-one-year-old woman with an enormous goitre on her neck, weighing at least one and a half kilos, and asked if we could take her to a hospital to have it removed. Back came her wonderfully astringent retort: 'What for?

I've lived with this thing hanging round my neck for so many years, I'm going to take it with me when I die!' It was typical of the feisty spirit of the people of Rangtse, who toil so hard to extract a living out of their land, which is on a steep slope.

The next morning—by a happy coincidence, it was Guru Padmasambhava's birth anniversary—I set off for Rangtse Ney. It took a knee-wrenching descent of an hour and a half to reach the cave, but my fatigue gave way to awe as soon as I arrived. The rocks at the entrance to the cave are red and shaped like tongues of fire— a phenomenon explained by the villagers as a miraculous manifestation of the Guru himself in the form of Dorji Droley (a form in which Guru Padmasambhava is surrounded by flames). There were pilgrims from all parts of Bhutan who had come to Rangtse on that auspicious day. Together, we offered prayers at a makeshift altar at the entrance and lit butter lamps fashioned out of hollowed bamboo stems. Then, donning a hard hat and carrying a torch, I entered the Rangtse Ney, a vast, silent cavern which can indeed hold a thousand people. But that was not all—at the back of the cave is a narrow tunnel which I was urged to explore. I crawled through this cramped, damp passage, which had stupa-like rock formations on its sides and emerged into another vast cave, known as the Cave of the Khandomas (angels).

Despite the fact that pilgrims have been coming to Rangtse Ney for centuries—my father had spent a week here in the 1930s—I was amazed at how immaculately clean both caves were, unsullied by the detritus of human encroachment. Whether the Rangtse Ney was created by an ancient geological upheaval or the Guru's miraculous powers, it exudes a powerful aura of unseen forces, both natural and divine, and no one who goes there can fail to be touched by it.

Set in a much gentler landscape is the great black rock of Gom Kora, in Tashi Yangtse district. One of the most sacred sites in eastern Bhutan—it is just 20 kilometres by motor road from the town of

Tashigang—this holy rock stands on the banks of a river in a tranquil oasis of green, lush with trees, paddy fields and banana groves. Legend holds that Guru Padmasambhava subdued an evil dragon which was terrorizing this area, and crushed it into the rock. The rock still bears the scars of that mighty battle: an imprint of the dragon's body and of the Guru's hat.

Guru Padmasambhava is also said to have hidden a *Tshebum*— a vase containing the water of immortality—inside the rock, and people believe that on very rare occasions, on auspicious days, this water can be seen trickling out of a crack in the rock. So you can imagine my elation when, on a family pilgrimage to Gom Kora, we saw water trickling down the rock as we circumambulated it, saying our prayers. We could scarcely believe our good fortune, when we spotted a man hiding inside the crack in the rock with a bucket of water—our King, whose spiritual beliefs are founded on rational thought, had devised this little joke at the expense of his gullible family!

For three days in the year, when the annual tsechu of Gom Kora takes place, this serene spot is transformed into a bustling makeshift township, which then vanishes without leaving a trace when the tsechu is over. Amidst the melee of people, livestock, tents and bamboo shelters, the semi-nomadic yak herders from the remote eastern valleys of Merak and Sakteng, and their close kin who come from Tawang in the Indian state of Arunachal Pradesh, stand out in their distinctive five-pointed black caps, red jackets and deerskin tunics (see Chapter 13). There are masked dances and special prayers during the tsechu, and lively trading of livestock, woven textiles and handicrafts. During the tsechu, devotees circumambulate the rock and its adjoining temple all through the night—and many romantic liaisons are made at this time. Youngsters living in small, cloistered communities in the remote interior of eastern Bhutan actually come to the Gom Kora Tsechu with the idea of finding a partner.

Among the items traded at the Gom Kora Tsechu is a particularly beautiful handicraft, a speciality of Tashi Yangtse district—these are the lustrous wooden lidded bowls known as *dapa*, which are used as serving dishes and plates, and which we Bhutanese prize more than the finest porcelain (these dapas can also sometimes be found at the weekly Saturday market in Thimphu). The dapas are made from the knotty burr or other such unusual growth on a tree trunk, as this part of a tree has an extraordinarily beautiful grain. The trees most favoured for making dapas are the red or white maple. According to traditional belief, eating from these dapas is not just good for the health, it can even ward off the effects of poisoned or contaminated food. The most prized dapas, proudly displayed as status symbols and treasured as family heirlooms, are those where the grain displays patterns like an owl's feathers; also coveted are those with the 'horses' teeth' and 'bamboo leaf' patterns. After being carefully collected from the forests in February and March, the wood for the dapas is specially treated and seasoned for four months, before being shaped on a pedal lathe. The bowls are then rubbed with the leaves of the *sogsogpa* shrub (*Trema poitoria*), which acts like a natural 'sandpaper' to make the surface smoother than silk, and then painstakingly polished with the leaves of the *sey* plant (*Rhus succedanea*) to give the dapas their wonderful golden patina. The entire process of dapa-making reflects the intimate knowledge of forest produce that so many people in Bhutan have, and the sustainable practices that are used in harvesting these resources, so that the deities of the forest are not offended.

Perhaps the single best place to see the wealth and variety of Bhutan's animals, birds and plant life is the Royal Manas National Park. Indeed, it is said to be the richest biodiversity spot in the entire Himalayas, and a model for the way in which its ecosystem has been preserved. It boasts 348 species of trees, 400 species of shrubs and herbs (many of great medicinal value) and nine species of rare orchids. The fauna includes forty-five species of mammals, including tigers, the one-horned rhinoceros and the golden langur, and over 350 species of birds, among them the rare rufous-necked hornbill, the pallas fishing eagle and the chestnut-breasted partridge. Ruling over this magical forest kingdom, which covers over 1000 square kilometres, are two powerful local deities, Tewaraja and Dewaraja, whose citadel is on a hill overlooking the park's guest house. The awe and reverence in which they are held ensure that all these plants and animals have an undisturbed habitat where they can flourish.

The Royal Manas National Park is contiguous with the Manas Tiger Reserve in India, a UNESCO World Heritage site (the Manas river forms the boundary between the two). Sprawling over two districts in southern Bhutan, Sarpang and Samdrup Jongkhar, Manas is a seven- or eight-hour drive from the foothills town of Phuentsoling in south-west Bhutan, crossing through the plains of India. It was a journey we did often, especially when the children were younger, to escape the winter chill of Thimphu for a few days and enjoy an idyllic family holiday in this balmy climate. Crossing the river by boat to enter the park, we would climb on to elephants and amble along the river to the guest house. This charming wooden house, its sky-blue ceiling painted with golden stars, and its garden stretching down to the river and a sandy beach, was built during the reign of the third king. It was here, too, that the present king spent his childhood winter holidays.

Our first act on arrival at the guest house was to offer a solemn ritual prayer to the deities of Manas, Tewaraja and Dewaraja. This puja would be performed with great dramatic flair by the king's old retainer, Ata Dophu, who would light butter lamps under a large tree at the edge of the lawn, lay out lavish offerings of food and recite prayers in a loud, sonorous voice, which always reduced us to giggles.

Every morning we would wake to the sound of birdsong, the soothing gurgle of the river and the sight of peacocks preening themselves on the lawn. Most mornings would be spent exploring the forest on elephant-back. From this high vantage point, we could reach out to touch the orchids festooning the trees, and admire the daring trapeze acts of the golden langurs as they jumped from tree to tree, eating the fruits of the forest and licking the nectar from the delicate mauve flowers of the bauhinia tree. Manas is one of the rare places where this beautiful animal, with golden fur framing its black face, can be seen. Another sight that thrilled us was that of the great pied hornbills, their distinctive raucous call echoing through the forest. The grasslands of Manas are equally exciting to explore—we have seen tigers and rhinos there, herds of wild elephants, buffalo and deer.

The banks of the river in front of the guest house were another spot where we would spend hours enjoying the cool breeze off the water, watching the antics of otters, the patient vigilance of kingfishers, and bison and elephants quenching their thirst, with herons and egrets perched companionably on their backs. We would look for tiny shrimp under the rocks and if we found enough there would be shrimp fried rice for dinner. All our children learned to swim here, and we became familiar with every twist and turn in the river as we took boats upriver to explore other, more secluded coves and beaches. As night fell, we would sit in the garden and watch the flying fox, a huge bat-like creature with a giant wingspan, the pied hornbills returning to their nests, the croaking of frogs and cicadas breaking the silence of the night.

Manas National Park, with its forests as old as time, where creatures great and small coexist, brings to life the familiar image of The Four Friends. And Parsuram, our boatman there, seems to epitomize the painting of The Six Longevities. Over the twenty years and more that we have been going there, Parsuram does not seem to have aged a day—like the old man in the painting, he lives in total harmony with the trees, animals and birds, the rocks and the clear running water of the Manas, and so seems to have discovered the secrets that allow him to defy time and age.

CHAPTER 6

THE HOT SPRINGS OF DUNMANG

Taking a cure at the hot springs is a favourite Bhutanese pastime, especially in the cold winter months. Apart from the fact that we set great store by their therapeutic effects, a visit to these springs—usually located in very scenic places—has all the delightful features of a week-long family holiday. I have been going to the hot springs since my childhood. As soon as my grandparents or parents would start making plans for their 'annual cure' at the Gasa hot springs in northern Bhutan, the whole household would excitedly begin preparations. Quantities of dried pork, beef and fish would be packed, together with eggs, butter, roasted corn, rice and casks of *chungkay*, a mildly alcoholic rice broth which is just the thing to have sitting round the campfire in the evenings, after spending the day soaking in the pools.

We would reach Gasa after a two-day trek from our home in Nobgang, along steep mule tracks which wound through deep forests. The atmosphere at the hot springs was most congenial. Everyone there would be completely relaxed, with no chores and no responsibilities, except to dip in the warm water, cook and eat—and the hot springs certainly made one very hungry! It was an opportunity for us as children to make new friends amongst families who had come from faraway places, while the elderly would be happily absorbed comparing notes about their respective ailments. There would be many unhurried, convivial evenings around the campfire. Soaking in the pools was not a priority for me then. It was many years later, when I was suffering from rheumatoid arthritis, that I discovered their remarkably beneficial effects, at another hot spring, far from Gasa, at Dunmang in central Bhutan.

The hot springs of Dunmang, though wonderfully picturesque, are precariously located on the narrow ledge of a cliff, in the Kheng region of central Bhutan, in Zhemgang district. From the pools at Dunmang, it is a vertical drop of almost a hundred metres down to the Mangdechhu river, which drones like a million honeybees as it charges over giant boulders on its way to Assam, where it joins the Brahmaputra.

In the mid-1990s I had been diagnosed with rheumatoid arthritis which caused me great agony, apart from nearly immobilizing me for long stretches of time. I then started treatment prescribed by the Bhutanese indigenous system of medicine (which I will write about in greater detail later in this chapter). For three years I took nine pills a day, made of thirty-two medicinal plants and flowers found in Bhutan, as well as minute amounts of gold, coral and other metals and minerals. The indigenous medicine considerably reduced the inflammation in my joints, especially in my fingers and wrists, but after a time the inflammation would come back. I even asked my doctor to get in touch with the Hollywood actor James Coburn, who had found relief for his rheumatoid arthritis from an alternative cure. He was kind enough to respond with his remedy. But before I could try it, I decided to go to the Dunmang hot springs, which I had heard were particularly efficacious for my affliction. There is a motor road up to Praleng, from where it is a one-hour trek to the hot springs. The old mule track to the hot springs is also still in use, and follows the course of the Mangdechhu river. Recently the track has been relaid to raise it, as parts of it always got submerged when the river was in flood. So the Dunmang hot springs are now much easier to get to than they were a few years ago.

There are four pools at Dunmang, the largest about three metres by two metres. Trees form a lush green canopy around and over the pools, screening them off to provide privacy. It is especially magical to soak in the pool in the evening, with the moon peeping through the broad leaves of the yikashing (*Aesandra butyracea*) trees, creating silvery reflections in the water. Steaming water, which gushes forth from cracks in the rocks around, is channelled into the pool and then drained off into the river below.

The water in the large pool is of a perfect temperature, warm and soothing. But the state of relaxation that soaking in the warm pool induces can be dangerous, for the ledge around the pools is so narrow that it leaves no room for a single false step. Some years ago two monks, their feet wet from the pool, slipped off the ledge and plummeted down to the raging river with its unforgiving currents. Their bodies were never found. During the monsoons there are other hazards. Rocks fall near the pools from the forested slopes above, sometimes dislodged by monkeys or mountain goats, and they have killed people in the past. Once a boulder fell right through the metal-sheet roof of the guest house, into a room—fortunately, the guest house now has a concrete slab roof. I myself had a narrow escape on my second trip to Dunmang—had I not been delayed at the road-head while transferring baggage from my car to porters and pack animals for the steep climb to the pools, I would have been squashed by a falling boulder. It was my destiny or karma that I reached the spot just minutes after the boulder had fallen.

Despite all these hazards, I have gone back to Dunmang three times, for the hot springs have completely cured me of my arthritis. I no longer need to take those nine pills a day or indeed any other medication. My blood tests, which had earlier confirmed the positive rheumatoid factor, showed negative results after my first visit to Dunmang. My later visits served as 'booster shots' to ensure I remain free of the disease. I have heard dozens of other stories of such cures at Dunmang, and I can bear personal witness to two of them—one, a trekking companion of mine, and the other a student at the Zhemgang high school, who had earlier had to drop out of school because the disease had nearly crippled her. I also know people who have been completely cured of chronic skin problems here.

Earlier, because of its remote location and lack of accommodation, not more than 500 people came to Dunmang every year. Now, with news of its remarkable cures spreading through the media, with easier access and better facilities such as a guest house and public toilets, the number of visitors to Dunmang has gone up four times in the last three years. People travel for several days to come here from all parts of the country in search of a cure. Space for expansion is limited on that steep cliff face, so to accommodate the growing number of visitors a new guest house is being built at Kamjong village, which is a steep two-hour walk uphill. But after a few hours spent soaking in the pools, that climb will, I'm willing to bet, feel as easy as a cakewalk!

While I was at Dunmang on my second visit, my mother was taking a cure at the Gasa hot springs, a familiar spot since my childhood. It used to be an easy two-day walk from our home in Nobgang, but now that the motor road has been extended, it takes only a day's walk from Punakha. Late autumn is the best season for Gasa. For one, the leeches that infest the trail during the monsoons are gone, and one can enjoy the spectacular scenery along the trail. The trail follows the Phochhu river, a sparkling torrent of jade-green water. The eighteenth-century English traveller, Captain Samuel Turner, who made the journey to the Gasa hot springs, describes the landscape en route, with its deep gorges and craggy cliffs, as 'Nature in its most gigantic and rudest form'.

Even in November, the forest is a delight, with the autumn-flowering wild cherry creating vivid splashes of pink, and the delicate mauve *Pleione praecox* orchid sprouting from the moss-covered branches of oak trees. The enchanting village of Goen Dhamji, with its handsome stone houses and terraced rice fields sweeping down to the river, is about halfway from Punakha to Gasa. In one of the houses, where Zhabdrung Ngawang Namgyel spent the night on his way to Gasa, are precious relics of his visit—a beautiful pair of brocade and leather boots, and an image of himself, made by his own hands, that he gave his hosts. Their descendants still live in the same house.

Another spot to look out for, on the outskirts of Goen Dhamji, is a vertical rock face with an intriguing-looking triangular opening in it that has been sealed by a stone. The legend goes that a demoness had been creating havoc in the area, until the saint Drukpa Kinlay arrived here, captured the demoness and imprisoned her inside the rock. I have to say that every time I pass this way my fingers itch to remove the stone that seals the triangular opening, and see if she's still in there!

A couple of hours before one reaches the hot springs, Gasa Dzong comes into view, against its backdrop of towering snow peaks and brilliant blue sky. From that distance it seems to float in the clear air, and is a truly unforgettable sight. Built in 1649 by Zhabdrung Ngawang Namgyel to guard the vulnerable frontier with Tibet, and later repaired and extended by Desi Tenzin Rabgye, Gasa Dzong is an architectural marvel, ingeniously built to follow the steep contours of the mountainside on which it stands. Particularly unique is the way its three courtyards rise in tiers, one above the other.

At the foot of the dzong flows the river, with the hot springs bubbling up along the riverside. Their steaming water is channelled to a series of large pools, each fed from a different spring, and each reputed to have different medicinal properties. There are, for example, different springs for those seeking relief from asthma, sinus problems, rheumatism and so on. Apart from its spectacular setting, I love the Gasa hot springs because they are perhaps the only ones in the world that have a separate pool for animals. It is always a delight to watch mules and horses soaking in their own hot pool in Gasa! A source of great amusement to the locals is the fact that foreign tourists trekking the popular Lingzhi–Laya route often head straight for the animals' pool since it is the largest and is empty when there are no animals in it—the Gasa villagers are too polite to disclose why no humans bathe in that pool. Captain Samuel Turner's eighteenth-century account of the hot springs asserts that 'none but the good and holy men are susceptible of its virtues, the profane who resort hither being incapable of enjoying its efficacy'. That was probably a myth spread by the monks to keep the hoi-polloi out. Today, the semi-nomadic yak-herding community of Laya claim the hot springs as their own and when they want the pools to themselves they just strip naked so that others leave in embarrassment. Older people who want to be in the pools by themselves also often use this strategy.

Among other things, the Gasa springs are renowned for their efficacy in lowering blood pressure. I once discovered, to my cost, quite how effectively they can do so. Having spent four days there with my parents and my children, spending long hours soaking in the pools, one night as I lay in my tent I had a strange out-of-body experience—I felt myself floating near the ceiling of the tent, watching myself sleep. It turned out my blood pressure had dropped dangerously low, and I had had what was probably a low-blood-pressure-induced hallucination. I had to be evacuated by helicopter from Gasa.

Another hot spring in a very beautiful place is Dur, in the northern part of Bumthang province, in central Bhutan. The Dur hot springs have the least number of visitors, because the entire journey has to be done on foot or on horseback, with no road-head nearby. From Jakar, the capital of Bumthang, it is a difficult two-day trek along a steep trail which crosses the high Gongtola Pass at 4327 metres and the Dyulela Pass at 4550 metres. To compensate, the trail is very scenic, thickly forested with juniper and other conifers, and in spring, the rhododendron forests along the route are absolutely spectacular, with many of the fifty varieties of rhododendron that Bhutan boasts in full bloom. One also passes several lovely alpine lakes en route.

The Dur hot springs are located on the upper course of the Mangdechhu river, though it is normally thought of as being at the head of Chamkarchhu river. And here, as at Dunmang, one has to watch one's step—one slip on the algae at the edge of the pool, and one could fall to one's death into the river. Water gushes out from underneath rocks and flows into eight pools at the Dur spa, which are reputed to be beneficial for thirteen different ailments. There are wooden shingle roofs over the pools and planks around them. Crystallized salt decorates the pool walls, sparkling in the sunshine and glowing in the dark, and creating the atmosphere of a fantasy-land wreathed in vaporous mists. I spent three blissful days at the Dur hot springs at the end of my arduous trek to the Lunana region. My favourite pool, fed by its own spring which bubbles up from the rocky bottom of the pool, was one where Guru Padmasambhava is believed to have bathed when he first came to Bhutan in the eighth century. The large footprint at the rim of the pool is said to be his, and the smaller one that of his consort. In the surrounding area one can see vapour rising from the forest, where there are hidden hot springs—a total of 108 sources, it is said. These have still to be explored.

For those who cannot go to the hot springs, there is the Bhutanese custom of taking a 'stone bath' which offers a cure that can be taken closer to home. The stone bath is taken in a wooden trough—and there are dozens of them scattered in every part of the country, close to springs whose waters are rich in minerals. One end of the trough has a separate section where heated stones are placed. The water from the medicinal spring is piped over the stones which heat the water and release their healing minerals. Soaking in a stone bath gives instant relief from aches and pains. Everyone has their own favourite place for taking stone baths. In the Thimphu Valley, for example, one can take a stone bath behind Dechenphug Monastery and at the base of Cheri Monastery. The wooden trough is already there—all you have to do is make a fire to heat the stones which can be found nearby, erect a little screen of pine branches for privacy and have a luxurious soak. I strongly recommend it! My editor at Penguin Books swears by the stone bath at Dobji Dzong, close to the Chhuzom (Confluence bridge on the Thimphu–Paro road)—it cured her of the frozen shoulder that had plagued her for years.

The use of natural ingredients for healing has long been part of the Bhutanese tradition. The ancient name for our country was Lho Jong Men Jong which means the Southern Land of the Medicinal Herbs, and Bhutan was the source for much of the raw material used in the traditional Tibetan as well as Chinese systems of medicine. The Bhutanese indigenous system of medicine, known as Sowa Rigpa, is similar to the Tibetan system, and its origins go back to the eighth century, when Buddhism was introduced to Bhutan and Tibet by the Indian saint Guru Padmasambhava. Because the alleviation of suffering is an essential part of the Buddhist faith, among the texts that the disciples of the Guru had translated into Tibetan were Indian medical treatises. These influenced the development of the Sowa Rigpa system of medicine, which later also absorbed influences from Chinese and Arab systems.

From Indian Ayurveda, the Sowa Rigpa system adopted the theory that human beings are composed of three humours—wind, bile and phlegm—and diseases result when these are destabilized. The destabilization could have many causes—the weather, negative emotions such as jealousy or anger, as well as evil spirits and one's actions in a past life. The treatment thus includes meditation and spiritual guidance as well as medicine. From Chinese medicine, the Sowa Rigpa system has borrowed the science of pulse-reading, which is far more detailed than pulse-reading in allopathic medicine.

It can detect diseases in any organ of the body, not just in the circulatory system and the heart.

Some 400 plants found in Bhutan, as well as minerals and a few animal parts, are used to make indigenous medicines. The medicinal plants, which make up two-thirds of the Bhutanese materia medica, are usually found at altitudes above 4000 metres, and include poppies, asters, delphiniums, hypericum (St John's Wort) and the rare and curious-looking *Cordyceps sinensis.* (*Cordyceps sinensis* is actually a kind of caterpillar on whose head grows a grass, which is especially prized in China as an elixir of life. Scientific tests have now confirmed that the *Cordyceps* has strong immunity-boosting properties.) The importance given to healing plants is even reflected in our iconography—the Buddha of Medicine is always shown with a terminalia plant in his hand.

The minerals used in indigenous Bhutanese medicine include gold, precious stones and several calcites and sulphurs, while the animal components traditionally included such exotic ingredients as bear bile, the gallstones of elephants and 'dragon bones' (which are actually fossils found in the high Himalayas). Thankfully, we no longer use animal parts such as rhino horn or musk, taken from endangered species—they have been substituted by plants with similar properties. Indeed, there is a rare high-alpine herb that smells exactly like musk-pods.

The plants and minerals are processed and mixed in a variety of combinations to make about 300 drugs in the form of pills, powders, lotions, infusions and syrups—all manufactured under conditions of strict hygiene and scientific standardization at the National Institute of Traditional Medicine in Thimphu. The institute, which runs a hospital, laboratories and a manufacturing unit in Thimphu, and a dozen dispensaries in different parts of the country, has a rigorous five-year training programme for doctors. Our traditional medicine is particularly effective for certain ailments, among them hypertension, digestive problems, allergies, rheumatism, insomnia and in building up immunity. But it does not offer surgery, and it cannot help in many acute conditions. The training of indigenous doctors, however, includes being able to diagnose quickly which patients need to be immediately referred to allopathic doctors—those suffering from cancer or tuberculosis, for example.

Indeed, the remarkable thing about the actual practice of indigenous medicine in Bhutan is the way in which it tries to integrate traditional and modern systems of medicine. So if you have, say, an acute allergic condition and come for a consultation to the Institute of Traditional Medicine in Thimphu, the *dungtsho* (doctor) there, after detailed pulse-taking and examination of urine and blood, may well send you to the allopathic hospital for a short course of treatment with antihistamines to begin with, and then call you back for a longer course of treatment with indigenous herbal pills, followed by a few days of soaking at the hot springs. It would be a good thing if allopathic doctors in the developed world were to have the same open-minded attitude towards traditional medicine systems based on medicinal plants and minerals.

CHAPTER 7

'I HAVE BEEN HERE BEFORE'

Of all the rites of passage, the Bhutanese regard funerals as the most important, because they mark not just the passing of a soul but the beginning of its journey into rebirth. Funeral rites last for twenty-one days, and are far more elaborate affairs than are birthdays and weddings. We believe that human beings go through many, many cycles of rebirth. We cannot predict when or where we will be reborn. But the quality and nature of one's next life can be determined, at least to some extent, by the merit one has accumulated over previous lives, through acts of piety, compassion and just simple everyday kindness. The most evolved human beings are those who through their great purity of heart and mind are finally freed from the cycle of rebirths and attain nirvana.

We also believe that the greatest saints and spiritual masters are reincarnated when they feel their presence is particularly needed. In order to be recognized as holy reincarnations, they manifest extraordinary gifts and feats from a very young age. Our belief in the reincarnation of saints and great lamas is a source of great comfort and hope. But it has also given rise, in our times, to a disturbing phenomenon—a profusion of false claims by individuals who conspire to have themselves declared the reincarnation of a particular holy figure. They then call themselves Rimpoches, set themselves up very comfortably in the 'holy business', enjoying great reverence and respect, and living off the generosity of gullible followers, including many from the West. We call them the 'Dollar Lamas'!

All this is by way of a prelude to two true stories I am about to tell you. The first recounts a personal experience which defies any rational explanation and the second describes the extraordinary discovery a few years ago of a reincarnation of one of the most revered figures in Bhutanese history.

When I was in my late thirties, I began to have a recurrent dream from which I would wake up with a lingering sadness, often finding my face wet with tears. Each time I would wonder why I was having this dream. My dream featured a big, three-storeyed traditional Bhutanese house, with a large covered balcony on the second floor. A slender, rather tall woman, perhaps in her late twenties, would be standing on the balcony with a sleeping toddler strapped to her back. The woman wore a kira, fastened at the shoulders by a pair of silver koma (traditional brooches) of a rather old-fashioned design. She had a haunting expression of sadness and yearning on her face, as though she was waiting for someone to return. Behind her on the porch sat two women weaving on the backstrap loom. The house had a walled courtyard with young orange trees laden with ripe fruit. At this point the dream would end. After this dream recurred several times, I began to feel that I was the woman in the dreams; I even experienced her emotions and her grief. In my dream I could feel the child's breath and warmth on me, as though I was the one carrying it.

One day I described the house of my dreams, with its walled courtyard full of orange trees, to my father. I asked him if he knew of any house that fitted this description in the orange-growing regions of Bhutan. 'Is the house in your dreams painted or unpainted?' asked my father. 'Painted,' I replied. 'Then the house in Shelgna Shingchum is the one,' said my father. 'I have been there and it fits your description exactly.' But I didn't believe the house from my dreams really existed.

Months passed. I continued to have the same dream. Then one day, in 1993—I was then thirty-eight—I decided on an impulse to go to the house in Shelgna Shingchum. The house was far beyond Punakha Dzong, across the Phochhu river. I walked through paddy fields for quite some time before the house came into partial view in the distance. I walked on towards it, and stopped at a *mani chukor*—a water-driven prayer wheel—to look at the house more closely. An uncanny feeling of déjà vu came over me. The house was identical to the one in my dreams. Behind the house stood a rather fine-looking woman, perhaps in her late fifties, with the closely cropped hair and maroon robes of a nun. She looked very familiar. 'We have met before, haven't we?' I said, as I stopped to greet her. 'No, we have not met before,' she replied, and then invited me into her house for tea. She had been born in that house, she told me, and now lived there with her son's family. She had become a nun after she was widowed, as is not uncommon in Bhutan.

As we climbed up to the second floor I looked out of a narrow window and saw a courtyard with just two gnarled old orange trees, with only a few shrivelled fruit on them. The wall around the courtyard had crumbled. Just bits of it remained intact at the corners, the rest strewn around as debris of mud and stone. A feeling of gloom overwhelmed me. My daughter, Sonam Dechan, who was with me asked what was wrong. 'It's the orange tree courtyard from my dreams—how has it become such a desolate ruin?' I whispered to her.

The nun, who had gone to bring us refreshments, now came back with butter tea and saffron rice. I sat silently, trying to compose myself and wondering whether I should take my quest further. Finally, I couldn't resist asking her: 'Did the mother of a little child in this house die young?' Her answer was prompt: 'My mother died when she was thirty-one, when I was three years old.' This fitted in with the ages of the mother and child in my dream. I asked her how her mother had died—she had died of smallpox, a killer in Bhutan in those days. The nun told me she remembered that her mother's body had been exhumed and cremated about a year after her death, as it was believed that the cremation of smallpox victims might spread the infection. All this had happened more than fifty years ago.

Could it be that the child I carried on my back in my dreams was now living right here in this house? I didn't say anything more to the nun, but asked her to show me the other rooms in the house. I met her granddaughters—bright, pretty girls. And I saw the covered balcony on the second floor, so familiar from my dreams. There were no weavers there now, but I saw the holes that had held the fixtures of their backstrap looms. The nun told me that in her childhood that's where the weavers would work. There was just one detail that was different—the balcony railings were of a different design from the ones in my dream. As though reading my mind, the nun volunteered the information that the old railings had been replaced some years earlier.

Finally we went up to the third floor, to the altar room with its images and scriptures. I prostrated three times before the altar and turned to leave, when I saw an old pair of brass binoculars lying on the window sill. I picked up the binoculars to see what they had in their sights and got a sharp jolt. For there, clearly visible, across the river and high on a hill was Nobgang—the village where I was born.

I bid farewell to the family of my past life—if indeed that was who they were—without telling them anything about my dreams. The dreams ceased from that very night. I have not gone back to Shelgna Shingchum, nor met anyone from that family again.

But the questions remain. Did the sad-faced woman in my dreams pray to be reborn in the beautiful hamlet of Nobgang that faced her village and her house? And was she indeed reborn in Nobgang, some twenty years after her death from smallpox? And is that how I came to be the 'mother' of a woman who was now about twenty years older than me and had grown-up grandchildren? Or could it be that my recurrent dreams were fuelled by memories buried in my subconscious? Could the amazing resemblance between what I saw in my dream and what I discovered at the house in

Shelgna Shingchum just be a series of rare coincidences? I still don't know what to make of my intriguing experience which defies any logical or rational explanation. I leave it to my readers to interpret it themselves.

The second story, unlike my personal experience, is not open to multiple interpretations. It is about the discovery in 1998 of a little boy who, after meeting a series of stringent criteria and tests, has been officially recognized as the reincarnation of Desi Tenzin Rabgye, who was the civil ruler of Bhutan from 1680 to 1694. Desi Tenzin Rabgye is a towering figure in Bhutanese history, whom we revere for his radiant spirituality, his strong and enlightened leadership, and his brilliant administrative abilities. During his fourteen-year reign Bhutan enjoyed peace and tremendous progress. Among his many achievements were the building of Taktsang Monastery in Paro (see Chapter 9) and the rebuilding of Tango Monastery in its present magnificent form in the Thimphu Valley. Both are among the most hallowed sites in the Himalayan Buddhist world.

I was fortunate enough to play a small part in the discovery of Desi Tenzin Rabgye's reincarnation. Every year, on the National Day of Bhutan, 17 December, the King and his family travel to a different part of the country to celebrate the event. It is an opportunity for him to interact closely with the people of that region, to see for himself how their needs are being met, and assess how development projects are progressing.

In 1998, we were at Kanglung in the Tashigang district in eastern Bhutan, for the National Day. As is usual on this occasion, the King first addresses a large public gathering, after which he and his family serve lunch to all the people there. This time, during the speech, I noticed a tiny monk sitting on the podium, and wondered who he was. He was very composed and well behaved for his age, which seemed to be not more than four years. After serving lunch to everyone, we headed towards the bamboo enclosure where we were to have lunch, when I saw the little monk still sitting on the podium, all alone. I took him by the hand and brought him to our enclosure, where the King was sitting on a folding chair. The little one let go of my hand and walked straight up to the King. Reaching up to grip the armrest of the chair he announced: 'I have something to tell you.' 'I'm listening,' replied the King.

'We have met before. You were very old, you had a long beard then, and I was very young,' the child declared. Amused, the King let the little monk continue.

'I built Taktsang on your orders,' he said, and added calmly, 'and now I want to go to Tango.'

'And why do you want to go to Tango?' asked the King.

'I've left my things there,' he replied. 'And besides, I have to meet my Norbu and my Ugay.' (We later learnt that these were the names of Desi Tenzin Rabgye's monk-attendant and close companion.)

'So you have been to Tango already?' asked the King.

'Yes—a long time ago. It was I who built Tango.'

All of us in the bamboo enclosure had gathered around to hear this extraordinary conversation between the King and the little monk. He was just four years old. And curiously, he spoke in Dzongkha, the language of western Bhutan, and not in his mother tongue Sharchopkha, which is spoken in eastern Bhutan.

'What are your parents' names?' the King asked.

'Tsewang Tenzin and Damche Tenzin,' he replied. (These were, as we later found out, not his own parents' names, but those of Desi Tenzin Rabgye's parents.)

Could the little monk have been tutored and made to memorize all these details? Yet he answered these and many other questions, which he could not possibly have anticipated, so spontaneously and simply. Soon word spread of this unusual little monk who spoke and acted like an old man. Already, at this young age, he had cataracts in his eyes and very poor vision. So did Desi Tenzin Rabgye, who was practically blind towards the end of his life.

The little monk was born in a humble family in Kanglung. One day the Lam Neten (head abbot) of Tashigang district came to Kanglung for a religious ceremony. The little monk, then just two years old, told his mother how sad he was that the abbot did not recognize him, as they had been close associates. The child then asserted that the abbot had been his scribe and they had been very fond of each other. Stories began to circulate about many curious things the child had said and done, and all the details he seemed to know about Desi Tenzin Rabgye, as well as all those who had been close to him.

These reports came to the notice of the Seventieth (and present) Chief Abbot of Bhutan, Je Khenpo Trulku Jigme Choeda. Soon after the little monk's meeting with the King, the Chief Abbot decided to find out more about the child. He sent one of the four principal monks in the Central Monk Body to examine the child. This senior monk was the Master of Dialectics, the Tsennyid Lopon—a fitting choice, as it was Desi Tenzin Rabgye who had established the discipline of dialectics (or philosophical debate) in the monastic body of Bhutan. From the moment the little monk met the Master of Dialectics, he refused to let him out of his sight—he was worried the Lopon would return to Thimphu and leave him behind, for he had set his heart on going to live in Tango Monastery. The little monk spent the night at the guest house in Tashigang with the Master of Dialectics, who was so impressed by his extraordinary intelligence, and the quiet aplomb with which he conducted himself, that he decided to take him to Punakha Dzong the next day, so that the Chief Abbot himself could meet the child. When they got into the car the next morning, his mother and sisters wept, but the four-year-old was completely fearless and composed as he left with a set of strangers, unaccompanied by a single person he knew.

It was a long journey to Punakha, with an overnight stop in Bumthang, but fortunately the child slept most of the way, only waking up when they had nearly reached Punakha, to ask: 'Have you got a white silk scarf with the eight auspicious signs on it that I must offer the Je Khenpo?' Everyone in the car was amazed that though he had never travelled this far before, he knew when they were approaching Punakha, and also precisely the kind of scarf that etiquette demanded he offer the Chief Abbot. Since they arrived at Punakha Dzong late in the evening, the Lopon took the child to his room to rest. But he immediately walked up to a mural on the wall, pointed to a building painted there and identified it correctly: 'This is Humrey Dzong.' The Tsennyid Lopon was taken aback—how did the child know? Humrey Dzong had been an important dzong in the seventeenth century, but not a trace of it now remained.

The next morning, 25 January 1999, the little monk met the Chief Abbot. He greeted him observing all the elaborate rules of etiquette that religious protocol demanded, and then watched the Sachoy Ritual which takes place on that day every year. Two top district officials were also there for the occasion, and the child observed that their sword scabbards were exposed. 'Cover them!' he instructed, following the rule that prevailed in the seventeenth century, but which no one observed in the twentieth century.

Having spent seven days at Punakha Dzong, during which he completely won over the heart of the Chief Abbot, the child travelled to Thimphu on the full moon day of the twelfth Bhutanese month—a particularly auspicious day. En route, he was asked if he had travelled this route before. 'Yes,' he replied, 'but the last time I came on horseback, otherwise I would not have felt so car-sick on this journey.'

While preparations were being made for the little monk to go to Tango, he stayed in my house for nine days. He applied monastic rules to my house, reminding me not to let other women and children into my house after dark. One day the Je Khenpo came to my house for an informal visit and, as I was about to lead him into the sitting room, the little monk suggested that it would be better to take him to the temple first. While we sat there, Zepon Wangchuck unexpectedly came in. Zepon Wangchuck, a former monk, was in charge of rebuilding Taktsang Monastery which had been destroyed in a fire in 1998. The little monk had never seen him before and did not know his name. Yet now he turned to him and said, 'Make sure you do a good job of rebuilding Taktsang. If you do it well I will give you a gift. And if not . . .' He gestured with his little hands to make it clear he would give Zepon Wangchuck a beating!

One day, soon after his arrival in Thimphu, my younger sister showed him a photograph of Tango Monastery and asked him if he recognized it. 'Yes of course,' he retorted, 'but I don't see Dzonkha in this picture.' At that time, none of us knew that Dzonkha was the name of the place above Tango where Desi Tenzin Rabgye used to meditate.

Tango Monastery, built in 1688, perches on the edge of a thickly forested hill at the northern end of the Thimphu Valley. It looks like a fortress of the gods, soaring towards the skies, with its great white semicircular wall gleaming amidst the lush greenery of the trees surrounding it. Enormous windows, framed in intricately carved and painted wood, break the starkness of its outer facade, which encloses a large stone-flagged courtyard. Covered arcades surround the courtyard, their walls painted with beautiful frescoes depicting deities, great saints and lamas. A short but steep flight of steps leads from the courtyard into the temples and the monks' dormitories.

Young monks in their red robes can always be seen milling around, for Tango is now Bhutan's main Buddhist institute, with 200 monks studying there. The hill on which Tango stands is surrounded by little meditation huts, and some of the senior students choose to go into solitary retreat here, traditionally for three years, three months and three days. During this time, the only person they see is their monk-tutor, who brings them food and keeps an eye on their health and welfare. It has to be said that only few are considered emotionally and mentally strong enough to be allowed to go into this long retreat—for it must be a hard thing to commune with one's innermost self for so long, without any other human contact.

On 20 March 1999, the little monk, whom I shall henceforth refer to as Desi, was carried in a palanquin procession to Tango. All along the way people lined the route to pay homage to him and witness this very special moment in our history. On reaching Tango, he prostrated before the altar in the main temple, and was then ceremonially enthroned as the reincarnation of Desi Tenzin Rabgye. He then turned to the principal of Tango, Kuenlay Gyeltshen, and hailed him as the reincarnation of Norbu, Desi Tenzin Rabgye's trusted monk-attendant. Later he would identify the reincarnation of his other close confidante, Ugay. As the little Desi climbed to the second floor of Tango, he stopped suddenly, entered a chamber and exclaimed, 'This is where I used to stay.' In the seventeenth century, that room was indeed the bedchamber of Desi Tenzin Rabgye.

The year 2005 marks the fifth year since the installation of Desi at Tango Monastery. Since he came to live there, electricity and telephone lines have reached Tango. After being tutored at first by one of the senior-most monks in the Central Monastic Body, the Dorji Lopon, his second tutor was a famous ascetic, Tsham Penjor, who had spent all his life meditating in caves in the mountains of Bhutan. Tsham Penjor was at first reluctant to become Desi's tutor, but then agreed to do so for one year—it was important that Desi be taught by a person with no attachment to material things.

Now ten years old, he presides with great dignity over all the rituals at Tango. He lives an austere life, gets up before dawn to start the prayers and enforces strict discipline among the monks in the prayer halls and during rituals. Almost daily, he goes alone into the dark inner sanctum of the Protecting Deity of Tango, Bayoeb, and spends ten minutes communing with him. He has the same quiet self-confidence as when I first saw him, and the same delightful sense of humour and fun, but is now more guarded and less spontaneous in his speech.

On 28 April 2005, Taktsang Monastery, the most sacred site in the whole of Bhutan, which had been destroyed in a fire and painstakingly rebuilt over seven years, was consecrated anew. The ceremony was conducted by the little Desi, the young reincarnation of the one who had originally built this monastery three centuries earlier. His presence on that momentous occasion seemed to have been ordained by the gods.

CHAPTER 8

DZONGS AND CHORTENS

Perhaps the first aspect of Bhutan that strikes a visitor on arrival is our unique architecture. Most Bhutanese buildings, even humble farmhouses, are beautifully harmonized with their natural surroundings. Typically, they display a superb sense of proportion and space, their simple lines and solid masonry offset by a gracefully pitched roof, and embellished by finely carved and painted woodwork. The most distinctive expressions of Bhutan's architectural tradition are dzongs and chortens, ubiquitous features of our landscape.

The dzongs, towering citadels of whitewashed stone, dominate every district centre in Bhutan. Some dzongs are situated in a commanding position on the valley floor, as at Thimphu and Punakha, but more often they look like 'Castles in the Air', occupying strategic sites on top of high ridges or spurs, with a panoramic view of the valleys around them. Outstanding examples of these are at Gasa in northern Bhutan, Wangdiphodrang in western Bhutan, Tongsa in central Bhutan, and Tashigang and Lhuentse in eastern Bhutan. Dzongs reflect the close enmeshing of the religious and the secular in the Bhutanese way of life. They were built as both defensive fortresses and monasteries, and still continue to house government offices as well as the monk body of a district. Most of our dzongs were built in the seventeenth century, though some have been built in recent years in newly created districts.

Each dzong in Bhutan has unique features, often determined by the contours of the site on which they are built, but by and large they follow a similar pattern. Several storeys high, and roughly oblong in shape, they enclose two or more courtyards paved with large flagstones. The courtyards are surrounded by pillared arcades leading into rooms, cloisters and large assembly halls. A tall central tower, known as the *utse*, separates the courtyards, and houses temples and chapels on each floor. The high outer walls of the dzongs taper outwards at the base, their severe facades broken by large windows on the uppermost floors, framed in carved and painted wooden frames. The roofs have wide eaves, supported by carved brackets, and are crowned by magnificent golden pinnacles. Most of Bhutan's largest and oldest dzongs were originally built at the orders of Zhabdrung Ngawang Namgyel and later extended by his successors. This network of dzongs throughout the country enabled him to control and unify the country.

The magnificent scale and proportions of our dzongs, the ingenious manner in which so many of them have been built to follow the curves of the ridges and mountaintops on which they stand, were achieved without the blueprints of trained architects— merely the expert eye of a master mason who would stand directing and supervising workers engaged in the construction. Incredibly, not a single nail was used in the construction of these great dzongs—just immaculately crafted tenon and mortise joints, which securely hold in place perfectly dove-tailed wooden beams, floors, doors, windows and staircases.

On a very different scale from the dzongs, but replete with religious and emotional significance, are the chortens, some 10,000 of which are dotted all over the country. A chorten (known as stupa in Sanskrit), is basically a receptacle for religious offerings or sacred relics. They are built for a variety of reasons—to honour a great king, saint or lama, to commemorate a departed soul, to ward off evil spirits or danger (which is why they are often built on mountain passes or steep cliffs) or to mark an important event or a great victory. If one walks past a chorten, one must do so keeping it on one's right, and walk round it in a clockwise direction—to do otherwise invites bad luck! And to break open a chorten, to steal the precious relics it contains, is regarded as a terrible sin, a desecration of all that we hold holy. Alas, we see increasing incidents of chortens. in isolated places being broken and robbed of their treasures, which then find their way to antique dealers in neighbouring countries.

Bhutanese chortens are of varying shapes—you can see the four most usual types on the drive from Paro to Thimphu, at the spot known as the Chhuzom or Confluence (where two rivers meet) where a group of four little chortens represent four typical forms. Chortens can also be of varying sizes, some even having chapels inside them, such as the Memorial Chorten in Thimphu built in memory of the third king of Bhutan. A few are built in the Nepalese style, with a hemispherical base topped by a tower with eyes painted on all four sides, such as Chorten Kora in Tashi Yangtse district or the Chendebji Chorten near Tongsa. But the most common form of chorten in Bhutan is the square chorten with a sloping roof over its four sides, and a broad red band called the *khemar* below the eaves (the red band on any building denotes its religious character). Carved slates depicting images of deities and Bodhisattvas are set into the khemar, and a gilded flame-shaped ornament crowns the roof.

Enter a dzong, and you will feel the reverberations of centuries of history—of the dramas, intrigues and great historical events that have taken place within its walls. Stand before a chorten and you can feel the powerful aura of protection that emanates from it. With a bit of imagination you can even smell the fragrance of the incense and herbs interred within, and hear the footfalls of the thousands of pilgrims who have circumambulated it with their prayer wheels and rosaries. All of us have our own favourite dzong and chorten, with which we have a special association. I will write here about just two dzongs, which are closely connected with the history of Bhutan and its monarchy, and a group of chortens that I built recently to mark an important event in Bhutanese history—an event that had a profound personal impact on me.

Perhaps the most majestic dzong in Bhutan is Punakha's Punthang Dechen Phodrang Dzong (the name means Palace of Great Bliss). Standing on a tongue of land where two rivers, the Phochhu and the Mochhu, meet, the dzong looks like a great ship at anchor. Punakha Dzong has a special significance in Bhutanese history. It was built in 1637 by Zhabdrung Ngawang Namgyel, the founder of the Bhutanese state, and it was here that the Zhabdrung died in 1651. His embalmed body is enshrined in the dzong's holiest temple, the Machen Zimchu, and all the kings and Je Khenpos of Bhutan begin their reigns by offering prayers at this shrine. Punakha Dzong was the place where Bhutan's first king, Ugyen Wangchuck, was crowned in 1907, after a hereditary monarchy was proclaimed by regional governors (penlops), state officials and representatives of the people and the monk body. It was here too that the first session of the National Assembly of Bhutan was held in 1952. In the winter months, the Je Khenpo and the entire Central Monk Body of Bhutan move from Thimphu's Tashichho Dzong to the more temperate climes of Punakha (the valley is at an altitude of 1250 metres), to take up residence in Punakha Dzong.

The site where the dzong stands had been a hallowed place long before the Zhabdrung's time. In the fourteenth century, the great Indian Buddhist saint Vanaratna, whom we call Ngagi Rinchen in Bhutan, had meditated here and built a little temple called the Dzongchung (little dzong), where he had placed a Buddha image. The image is still there, and though the Dzongchung has been damaged in floods many times and rebuilt, the flood waters have always miraculously stopped just short of the altar on which the Buddha image is placed. Not surprisingly, this serene and indestructible Buddha is an object of great devotion, and the Dzongchung is always thronged by pilgrims from all over Bhutan. A few kilometres away from the Dzongchung is an enormous rock with a large crack through it, which is equally revered as a sacred site. It is said that Ngagi Rinchen split open this boulder through the power of his prayers, to release the soul of his mother, which had been trapped here in the form of a frog. My father has built a tiny temple beside this rock, the Do Jagar Lam temple (the temple of the Indian saint's rock).

When Zhabdrung Ngawang Namgyel built the Punakha Dzong, he was fulfilling a prophecy made by Guru Padmasambhava in the eighth century. The Guru prophesied that a young man named Namgyel would come to the mountain that looks like a sleeping elephant, and build a dzong at the place where the tip of the elephant's trunk rests. If you look with your eyes and mind wide open, you will see that the mountain behind the dzong does indeed look like a sleeping elephant, whose trunk forms the land on which the dzong stands. The plan of the dzong was the work of a humble carpenter called Balep. The Zhabdrung instructed him to sleep in the Dzongchung, before the Buddha image, and Balep saw the design for the dzong in his dream. The dzong is 180 metres long and 72 metres wide, and its walls, made of stone masonry, are nearly two metres in thickness. According to legend, many deities of the Punakha Valley helped in the construction of the dzong. The Protecting Deity of my village, Nobgang, together with a female deity called Dorichum (the Lady of the Stones) created a landslide which delivered all the stone needed for the construction. The Protecting Deity of Tsachaphu, another nearby village, provided the timber, which he floated down the Phochhu river.

To approach the dzong, one must cross a suspension bridge over the Mochhu river. Every time I cross this bridge, memories come flooding back of my childhood visits to the dzong, accompanying my maternal grandmother, Ugay Dem. Our home, Nobgang, was just a two-hour walk from the dzong, and she would come every few months to meet the district officials on some work, or to call on a lama she revered. Then, as now, one had to be properly dressed to enter a dzong—head uncovered, men with a three-metre-long kabney (scarf) draped over the left shoulder and knotted at the side, and women with a shorter woven sash with fringed ends called a *rachu* draped over their left shoulder. The colour of the men's kabney indicates their rank—while private citizens wear white kabneys, a red one is worn by senior officials, an orange one by ministers, a kabney with a blue stripe by *chimi*s (National Assembly members), and white with red stripe for gups (county headmen). The King and the Je Khenpo wear saffron-yellow kabneys. Senior officials and ministers must also wear their ceremonial swords when they enter a dzong.

On my childhood visits, the bridge leading to Punakha Dzong was a great meeting point for people of the region. It would be crowded with people from neighbouring villages who would come here to sell their produce—fresh vegetables, peaches, pears, tree tomatoes, cucumbers and boiled cobs of corn. They would bring along a packed lunch and spend the entire day here, exchanging news and gossip. At the end of the day they would buy salt, tea and batteries for their torches from the few small shops near the dzong bridge, before trudging back home.

The bridge leads to a steep wooden staircase, seven metres high, above which is the great front door of the dzong. The staircase was designed so that it could be removed in times of war, making the dzong virtually impregnable. The front door leads to the first courtyard, which houses the district administration. At the end of this courtyard is the six-storeyed central tower, the utse, with temples on every floor, and superbly carved and painted windows. Notice how the walls of the utse slope outwards at the base, while the great windows start off widest at the top and get narrower near the base, giving the structure a marvellous balance and sense of lightness.

Bhutan's most sacred relic, the Rangjung Kharsapani (a self-created image of the Bodhisattva of Compassion, Avalokiteswara or Chenrezig), is kept in one of the utse's chapels. It was to recover this relic that the Tibetans invaded Punakha in 1639, and were defeated thanks to a clever ruse by the Bhutanese. The annual Punakha Domchoe festival, which I have described in Chapter 2, is held to celebrate this famous victory. Another temple in the utse houses the embalmed body of the Zhabdrung's son, Jambay Dorji. On the final day of the Punakha Domchoe, the great thongdrel (a gigantic silk banner) is hung, covering an entire outer wall of the utse. Measuring 28.3 metres by 25.2 metres, the thongdrel is a superb example of appliqué work and embroidery, and took more than fifty artists two years to complete, using 6000 metres of silk brocade. The central figure is that of the Zhabdrung, surrounded by other great religious figures of Bhutan.

Beyond the utse is the second courtyard, which is for the monks. It is surrounded by prayer halls, cloisters and several temples. Among them is the Dechog Lhakhang, where our formal wedding ceremony was held in 1988. The sound of chants and prayers, gongs and bells fills this courtyard from early in the morning. So too does the laughter and chatter of boisterous little monks letting off steam during their study breaks.

Punakha Dzong is unusual in having three courtyards, and the third courtyard, at the southern end of the dzong, boasts its architectural masterpiece, the enormous Kunrey, or assembly hall of the monks, with its fifty-four magnificent pillars. At the centre of this hall is a towering statue of the Buddha, flanked by images of Guru Rimpoche and the Zhabdrung. The Je Khenpo's living quarters and temple are situated here as well.

At this end of the dzong too is the Machen Zimchu, the temple where the embalmed body of the Zhabdrung is kept in a sealed casket inside a spectacular gilded chorten. As I have mentioned earlier, the Zhabdrung's death in 1651 was kept a secret for over forty years, for fear that news of his death would plunge his newly founded nation into instability. The people were simply told that the Zhabdrung had gone into meditation and would not appear in public. The ruse was successfully kept up by the Zhabdrung's heirs and those holding the reins of government, by food being taken into his chamber every day, and a slate with what purported to be his written orders emerging from time to time. Only the King and the Je Khenpo are allowed inside the Zhabdrung's shrine chamber, apart from two senior attendant monks who are caretakers of the shrine. In the same temple is the embalmed body of the saint Pema Lingpa (1450–1521) from whose lineage the kings of Bhutan are descended (however, there is some controversy about this as some believe it is the body of Pema Lingpa's son that is kept here).

Punakha Dzong has been ravaged by fire, earthquakes and floods many times, and then rebuilt according to the original design. The dzong suffered great damage in an earthquake in 1897, and the last great fire was in 1985, when the Je Khenpo's living quarters were damaged—dzongs are particularly vulnerable to fire, with their extensive use of wood, and the thousands of butter lamps that are lit every day in their temples. The most recent flood was in 1994, when a glacial lake in Lunana burst its banks because of unseasonably warm weather, creating a flash flood in the Phochhu river in Punakha, which swept away twenty-three people near the dzong and severely damaged parts of it (see Chapter 12).

After the fire in 1985, the King launched a major restoration of the dzong, and over the next eighteen years the Machen Zimchu, the monks' assembly hall and the Je Khenpo's quarters were rebuilt. The work was done using the traditional materials and techniques. This massive restoration project provided the impetus for a renaissance of the thirteen classical arts of Bhutan, collectively known as the *Zorig Chusum*. These include woodwork; stone arts (such as dressing stone and building walls); carving on slate, stone or wood; clay arts (including the making of religious images); bronze casting; blacksmithy (which includes sword-making); gold, silver and copper work; cane and bamboo basketry and thatch work; paper-making; weaving; embroidery and appliqué work. The very finest examples of all these arts can be seen in Punakha Dzong.

The consecration ceremony of the renovated dzong, held on 15 May 2003, was an event of memorable splendour. The Palace of Great Bliss, so lovingly and painstakingly restored, had never looked more beautiful, as it stood framed against a row of jacaranda trees in full purple bloom, against a brilliant blue sky, encircled by two sparkling rivers, and wrapped in the fragrance of incense and juniper smoke.

If Punakha is Bhutan's grandest dzong, the most charming is Wangdicholing. From the mid-nineteenth century, when a long period of civil wars came to an end and a more peaceful era dawned in Bhutan, some smaller dzongs were built, to serve more as family residences of the nobility than as defensive fortresses. Wangdicholing Dzong, in Bumthang district's Jakar Valley, is the finest example of these. Built in 1856 by the Tongsa Penlop Jigme Namgyel, the father of the first king of Bhutan, Wangdicholing Dzong was the seat of Bhutan's first and second kings, and the place where the third king, Jigme Dorji Wangchuck, grew up and served his apprenticeship in statecraft.

Jigme Namgyel selected an auspicious site for the construction of his new family home—the broad, green field on which he had pitched camp for his victorious battle against the governor of Jakar Dzong. His master mason, Zowo Gyenden, designed a building that harmoniously combined the grandeur of a dzong with the comfort and intimacy of a family home. A long, tree-lined driveway flanked by meadows leads to Wangdicholing's imposing entrance, with its great door, carved casements and beautiful murals. The large courtyard inside is surrounded by rooms on three floors—the ground floor rooms were used as storerooms, while the family rooms were on the first floor. At the top, under the eaves, were the rooms from where the king's secretaries and chamberlains worked. The family rooms are enchanting, their ceilings and walls painted in glowing colours. Each room has a different colour scheme—yellow and blue, orange and white, coral and green. Pillared recesses add charm and intimacy to these large spaces.

At one end of the courtyard is the utse—the three-storeyed central tower, with chapels on each floor. Jigme Namgyel's personal chapel is particularly beautiful. Two pairs of elephant tusks flank the three-tiered altar, lacquered in mellow red and gold. The copies of the holy scriptures kept here have sumptuous wooden covers embossed in gold.

There are vivid descriptions of life at Wangdicholing during the reign of the second king, Jigme Wangchuck, in the book *Hero with a Thousand Eyes* by Karma Ura. The monarch's day began at 6.30 a.m. with the royal astrologer announcing the forecast for the day.

Then came breakfast, after which the head chamberlain reported the list of visitors seeking audience and the gifts they had sent—these ranged from textiles to large hogs. Each gift was carefully assessed so that gifts of similar value could be reciprocated. At 9 a.m. a brass band would strike up in the courtyard, after which people would begin to file in for their audience with the king. Five secretaries toiled on the top floor, recording orders and decrees, dealing with correspondence and receiving petitions. The king's day ended at 10 p.m., when he finally took off his ceremonial sword and retired to bed.

An army of retainers was in attendance at Wangdicholing. Karma Ura's book lists 150 *changaps* (butlers, valets and men-in-waiting), five *kadreps* (conversation companions chosen for their wit and learning), forty *chandaps* (security squad), fifteen *chashumis* (personal aides whose tasks included helping the king mount his horse or walk downhill), eight chefs, some 200 *zingaps* (menial task force), twenty silversmiths, thirty blacksmiths, thirty weavers, twenty stablemen and the twelve-man brass band whose repertoire included Scottish airs on the bagpipes. Crown Prince Jigme Dorji Wangchuck served a strict apprenticeship at his father's court, which included learning the duties of an ordinary changap.

One of the highlights of the year at Wangdicholing, introduced by the second king, was an annual fair held in the dzong's grounds, which was attended by thousands of people from all over Bhutan. Its attractions included a lottery with livestock given as prizes, an archery tournament in which the king was an enthusiastic player, and a film show—each year, it was the same film, about a fight between a tiger and two dogs, but it never failed to enthral. Another novelty introduced by the king, which proved an instant hit with the people, was the game of musical chairs. The grand royal feast served during the fair included two prized Bhutanese delicacies—crisply fried wasps and golden hornets.

In the winter months, the court would move from Wangdicholing to Kuenga Rabden Dzong in the more temperate and sheltered Mangdelung Valley in Tongsa district. The three-day journey on foot was a massive exercise in planning and logistics, in which 500 courtiers and retainers, 300 porters and 100 packhorses were involved. The king would leave Wangdicholing in ceremonial procession, riding his favourite steed, the handsomest changaps walking beside him. The procession would be led by a drummer, a bell-ringer, a pair of *jaling* (oboe) players and, of course, the brass band.

After the death of the second king in 1952, the court moved for a while to Paro and then to Thimphu, which the third king declared would be the new capital. Wangdicholing Dzong lay empty for many years, but is now being restored for use as a family residence once again.

Chortens are minute in size as compared to dzongs, but they are far more potent in terms of their religious symbolism. Their simple exterior is in sharp contrast to the riches that are concealed within. A chorten is a manifestation of deep faith, and a humble act of devotion on the part of the person who has built it. In 2003, I undertook the building of a group of 109 chortens, at a time when our country and our King were faced with grave danger.

For nearly a century and a half Bhutan had not faced an external enemy—the last time the country had gone to war was in 1864-65, when the father of the first king, Tongsa Penlop Jigme Namgyel, had routed the British in the Duar War. Since then, we had perhaps become complacent, and taken for granted our peaceful, stable lives. But now, in 2003, war clouds were gathering. Militant groups from India's north-eastern region had established their guerilla camps in the dense jungles of southern Bhutan, from where they would launch terrorist attacks across the border. For many years our government and the King had held talks with these militant groups, trying to persuade them to leave Bhutan, and to stop using our territory to attack a country which was Bhutan's staunch friend. After six years of these futile negotiations, it became clear that the militants were not going to leave, that they posed a real threat to Bhutan's own security, and that armed action was unavoidable to expel them from Bhutan. Public opinion in support of this action had gradually been building up through discussions in the National Assembly and public meetings in all parts of the country. But no Bhutanese of our generation, or even that of our parents, had ever experienced the reality and the horror of war.

In late summer of that year, I noticed that my son, Jigyel, had been getting up at dawn each morning, and thought he was preparing for the rigours of academic life at Oxford, where he was to go that fall. I should have guessed from his tanned, slimmer frame and crewcut that those early mornings were spent not poring over books but in rigorous physical training. I only found out later that he had signed up to join the militia without telling me or his father, for fear that I would say no. In the event, Jigyel deferred his studies at Oxford for a year. Meanwhile, sharing the anxiety of every Bhutanese at this time, I started building a chorten at the Dochula Pass, as a visible symbol of my fervent prayers to the deities to protect our country at this difficult time.

On 4 December 2003, the King and Jigyel left Punakha for the battlefront. As my son got into the car with his father, he said to me, 'The war must not be lost by those who are left behind'—his way of telling me that we who were not soldiers must not give way to fear and panic, and must keep our spirits up. His parting words to me were that I should be prepared not to see him again, for if the worst were to happen to his father, he too would not come back alive from the battlefield. I knew he meant every word of it, and I told my son to do what he must.

My heart felt as heavy as a round river stone as they left, and I thought of all the other mothers, wives and children of soldiers in Bhutan, who would be experiencing the same anguish. The King travelled towards the south, addressing public gatherings on the way, ensuring that the armed forces were adequately equipped and trained, meticulously planning every detail of the logistics and strategy for the battle to come. He had no intention of issuing orders from Thimphu—his place was on the battlefield, beside his soldiers, he told them, for he regarded them and every Bhutanese citizen as his own children. They knew that these words came from his heart.

The day the King and Jigyel left Punakha I returned to Thimphu and went straight to Cheri Monastery, high on a mountain at the northern end of the Thimphu Valley. I climbed as fast as I could, to reach the cave above the monastery where the Zhabdrung, the founder of our nation, had meditated for three years. In the silence of that cave I felt the Zhabdrung's blessings and reassurance that all would be well, and left Cheri with a lighter heart, and a clearer idea of what contribution I could make, at a time when the future seemed so uncertain.

I lost no time in galvanizing the Tarayana Foundation, which I had set up in May 2003, to take the lead in coordinating civilian efforts. Within hours, thousands of volunteers had joined us in our efforts to help organize blood donations, set up a blood bank database and make plans for the rehabilitation of villagers who might be displaced from their homes near the battlefield. Cash donations came pouring in.

With the relief effort under way, I set off for the Dochula Pass on 6 December to fulfil another vow I had taken at Cheri Monastery. I climbed the snow-covered hillock to the chorten I had built, and there I pledged to build 108 chortens around it, as symbols of my prayers for the safe return of our King and our soldiers. (A hundred and eight is an auspicious number for Buddhists, representing the number of prayers that make up a complete cycle.) We began drawing up plans for the chortens that very day.

Before any chorten is built the ground has to be purified, and so on 8 December, the Je Khenpo came to perform this ritual, called the *senem kurim*. At various stages in the construction of a chorten, certain prescribed rituals and prayers must be held for it to serve its purpose effectively, and so it was with each of the 108 chortens that now simultaneously began to take shape. Once a chorten reaches the height of about one metre, an opening is made in the ground and symbolic offerings, such as grains and a bronze vessel filled with butter, are put in. The construction then proceeds until the next stage, when clay images of our deities, their hollow insides filled with handwritten prayers, are interred.

A vital stage in the building of a chorten is the installation of the *sokshing* or the 'life tree' of the chorten. The sokshing, which symbolically links heaven and earth within a chorten, is a long wooden pole, square in section, cut from a juniper tree by a person with the right astrological qualities. The pole is then painted red, prayers are written along its length in gold on all four sides, and sacred objects are tied to it—gilded images of deities, prayers bells, small clay stupas, prayer books, sachets of medicinal herbs and incense, as well as precious stones and jewellery. The sokshing is then covered with silk, and installed in the partially built chorten on an auspicious day. I took part in the prayers while the sokshings were being installed, tied with dozens of the most beautiful and sacred objects that had been offered for this purpose by different generations of the royal family.

I was overwhelmed by the generosity of countless other people, as well, who wanted to contribute to the building of these chortens. Cash as well as contributions in kind poured in from people in all walks of life—monks and engineers, students and housewives, officials and pensioners, farmers, masons, carpenters, image makers, slate carvers and craftsmen specializing in intricate brasswork. They toiled almost round the clock—to participate in the building of these chortens was an expression of their solidarity with the King and the army, as they faced what everyone feared would be a protracted and bloody war, against an enemy so skilled in guerilla warfare that even the mighty Indian army had been unable to defeat them.

It is not my intention here to write an account of the second Duar War of 2003—that is for future historians to do. It is enough to say that Bhutan's tiny army under the direct leadership of the King brought the war to an incredibly swift and conclusive end. In just one and a half days, between 15 and 16 December, the thirty camps established by the militants over fourteen years were destroyed by our army; many of their leaders were captured, and others fled to India.

But there was no crowing over victory, no jubilant victory celebrations—that is not our way. We mourned the eleven Bhutanese soldiers who died, and we lit lamps and offered prayers too for the militants who were killed, that their souls may find peace.

By the time the King returned to Thimphu on 28 December, the 108 chorten structures were just beginning to take shape. We had to stop work in January and February because of the bitter cold and snowfall on the Dochula Pass, but we resumed in full swing in early March. By mid-June, in what must be record time, all the chortens were ready. We named them the Druk Wangyel Chortens, or Chortens of the Victory of the Druk Gyalpo.

The consecration and sanctification ceremonies took place on 19 and 20 June 2004, in the presence of thousands of people, including the King. The 108 new chortens, in three tiers of forty-five, thirty-six and twenty-seven circling the main chorten, presented a magical sight. Each one was festooned with brilliantly coloured silk hangings, while on the ridge above them a veritable forest of prayer flags fluttered and flapped in the breeze. As we circumambulated the chortens at a particularly significant moment during the prayers, a ray of sunshine burst through the clouds and a rainbow emerged to encircle the Druk Wangyel Chortens. It seemed like a sign from the heavens—a sign that the Protecting Deities of Bhutan had arrived to witness the event, bless the chortens, and renew the faith and devotion of all those present.

PART THREE

PEOPLE
AND
PLACES

His Majesty King Jigme Singye Wangchuck on tour in rural Bhutan

Wedding portrait: (from left to right) Ashi Tshering Yangdon, Ashi Tshering Pem, the King, the author, and Ashi Sangay Choden

The author's parents, Yum Thuiji Zam and Yab Ugyen Dorji

His Royal Highness Crown Prince Dasho Jigme Khesar Namgyel
Wangchuck with the King

The Crown Prince, centre, with the author's daughter and son,
HRH Ashi Sonam Dechan and HRH Dasho Jigyel Ugyen

Taktsang Monastery, Paro, 1997

Blue poppies, the national flower of Bhutan, grow beside an alpine lake in north-western Bhutan

A scene from Royal Manas National Park, a haven for the rare golden langur, hornbills and elephants

An archery match at Nobgang village. The author's childhood home is
seen in the background.

A typical scene from the author's journeys on foot through the most remote
parts of the country

Punakha Dzong in its magnificent setting, encircled by two rivers

The Druk Wangyel Chortens at Dochu La

A Brokpa family and their yak. The village of Sakteng in eastern Bhutan is seen in the background.

Laya women at their encampment in northern Bhutan

Warriors in traditional dress and monks greet the arrival of Druk Air planes in Paro. Paro Dzong is seen in the background.

Paddy fields surround the historical temple at Nabji, central Bhutan

The author meets villagers under an ancient cypress tree in Dagana,
south-west Bhutan

A portrait of Zhabdrung Ngawang Namgyel (1594–1651), revered as
the founder and unifier of the Bhutanese state

The young Desi, recognized and enthroned as the reincarnation of Desi Tenzin
Rabgye, fourth temporal ruler of Bhutan (1638–96)

CHAPTER 9

PILGRIMAGE IN PARO

The Paro Valley is usually the visitor's first introduction to Bhutan. As the Druk Air flight soars over deep gorges and steep hillsides, a sudden opening in the wall of mountains reveals a wide and verdant valley, with a silver river winding through it. If you arrive in spring or summer, the valley is an emerald green patchwork of paddy fields, patterned with the softer green of the willows along the river banks. Fruit orchards around the farmhouses are a cloud of pink and white blossom, and the hillsides cloaked with flowering rhododendron and wild roses. In autumn the colours are equally spectacular—fields of golden paddy, framed by the vivid blue of the wild plumbago bushes, the deep pink of wild cosmos and the bright scarlet of chillies drying on grey shingled rooftops.

As spectacular as its natural beauty is Paro's cultural and spiritual heritage. With its large, fertile and well-watered fields, this has historically been the richest area in the country, and much of its wealth has gone into the building of temples and monasteries—there are many as 155 of them in Paro district. And it is a custom among the people of Paro to spend a week walking from one temple to the other, starting with the temples on the valley floor and then going up to the hills and highland meadows which are dotted with some of Bhutan's most holy sites. In the spring of 2001, I decided to do just that—go on a week-long pilgrimage to as many of the temples of Paro as I could manage.

I began with the Paro Tsechu, held at the majestic Rinpung Dzong. A traditional cantilevered and covered bridge leads across the river into the dzong, which houses some of the finest examples of Bhutanese religious art. Among them are cosmic mandalas and a towering Buddha statue in the monk's assembly hall whose exquisite face was modelled by my father's grandfather, Kuenga Gyeltshen.

The spectacular masked dances and processions attract many foreign visitors to the Paro Tsechu. But for me the most magical part of this festival is to go to the dzong before dawn, and wait quietly in the dark until the first rays of the sun gently touch the giant thongdrel (silk banner) of Guru Padmasambhava, which covers an entire wall of the dzong. That dramatic moment, when the rising sun first lights up the Guru's eyes, is when one experiences the sacredness of the occasion and the Guru's sublime blessings.

Just below the dzong is Paro airport—the only airport in our country—surrounded by fields, handsome farmhouses and a fast-growing township, with shops and hotels. Flights to Bhutan started as recently as 1986, but despite having discovered air travel only twenty years ago, the Bhutanese are now enthusiastic jet-setters. Druk Air flights out of Paro are full through the year with a wide cross-section of seasoned Bhutanese travellers—monks on the way to Kathmandu, traders to Bangkok, elderly pilgrims to Bodh Gaya, prosperous farmers to Calcutta and Dhaka to explore new markets for their delicious asparagus, mushrooms and strawberry, students and officials to Delhi. Yet, there is a special Bhutanese flavour to our jet age. Most Druk Air passengers have first consulted a religious almanac or a monk to ensure that they do not travel on an inauspicious day. And if air travel on such a day is unavoidable, we have a typically pragmatic solution—we make a symbolic start to the journey a day earlier, by packing our luggage and leaving home with it for a short while.

Close to the airport is one of Bhutan's oldest religious sites—the seventh-century Kyichu Lhakhang. It is said to be one of the 108 temples built by the Buddhist king of Tibet, Songtsen Gampo, to subdue a demoness who sprawled across the entire Himalayan region and prevented the spread of Buddhism. The temples were built to pin down different parts of her body, and Kyichu Lhakhang was built over her left foot (Jamba Lhakhang in Bumthang is said to pin down her left knee). In the eighth century this temple achieved even greater sanctity when Guru Rimpoche came to meditate here.

Prayer wheels are set all along Kyichu Lhakhang's outer walls, with lines of devotees turning them as they circumambulate the temple. Those who have been doing this for a long time achieve it at breathtaking speed, turning the wheels, chanting and counting their rosary beads all at the same time! The statues of the Bodhisattvas and of the Buddha in the sanctum of the temple are national treasures, and the wooden floor in front of the sanctum, set with large turquoise and coral gemstones offered by devotees, has little hollows where it has been worn down by the centuries of prostrations made before them.

Adjoining the old temple is a second temple built by Her Majesty the Queen Mother, Ashi Kesang Choden Wangchuck, in 1968. The two temples with their graceful golden spires now form a harmonious whole. Every year our family gathers at the new temple for the annual *Drupchen* prayers that the Queen Mother holds, for the well-being of the country and its King. In his lifetime, these annual prayer ceremonies were presided over by one of Bhutan's most revered spiritual figures, His Holiness the late Dilgo Khentse Rimpoche, whose blessings we were privileged to receive.

On top of the hill facing Kyichu Lhakhang is Sangchoekor Monastery, the seat of my father's late brother, the Speech Incarnation of the Zhabdrung. Just below it, on the same hill, is Kuengacholing, the mansion built by my father's grandfather, where my father was born. Much of my father's family history is associated with these two structures, which are outstanding examples of traditional Bhutanese architecture.

Paro's most famous site, of course, has always been Taktsang (Tiger's Nest) Monastery, a cluster of temples clinging to the edge of an impossibly steep and rocky cliff, seeming to hang in space some 800 metres above the valley. Visiting Taktsang in 1905, Sir

John Claude White, the British Political Officer in Sikkim, wrote: 'It was unquestionably the most picturesque group of buildings I had seen. Every natural feature in the landscape had been taken advantage of, and beautiful old trees . . . combined with the sheer precipices, made a magnificent picture.'

The site owes its sanctity to the belief that Guru Padmasambhava came here in the eighth century flying on a tiger, and meditated in a cave. Other great saints, such as Dorji Lingpa and Milarepa, have also meditated at Taktsang, which is revered throughout the Buddhist world. The steep and narrow path along the cliffside (a two-to-three-hour walk) to this sacred spot was one that I took each time I came to Paro, but in 2001 I could not include Taktsang in my pilgrimage. In 1998, Taktsang was destroyed in a fire, the cause of which remains a mystery. The caretaker monk was burnt to death, the precious religious images and relics charred to cinders, centuries of art, history and tradition consumed swiftly by the flames. Only the temple housing the Protecting Deity of Taktsang, Singye Samdu, was spared.

It was a defining moment in our history—most Bhutanese remember where they were and what they were doing when they heard this shocking news. We were far from Paro, touring Zhemgang in central Bhutan, and the news hit me like a physical blow. But this story has a happy ending—Taktsang has risen from the ashes. It has been painstakingly rebuilt, exactly as it was, with almost every Bhutanese citizen contributing to its reconstruction, in cash or in kind. The charred remains of the precious old images have been interred in the new images that have been made. It was a very special day in our history when the new Taktsang Monastery was consecrated on 24 March 2005, a symbol of Bhutanese resilience and faith.

But since in 2001 Taktsang was still being rebuilt, I went from Kyichu to the tall fort-temple of Zuri instead, an easy half-hour's walk from the National Museum above the dzong. Here is a corner of Bhutan that has remained almost untouched by the modern world since Zuri was first built in 1352. The site of Zuri was important long before this, as Guru Rimpoche had come here and blessed the ground. In the late ninth century a Tibetan prince, Lhasey Tsangma, who had been banished by his brother Langdharma (the heretical king of Tibet who wanted to stamp out Buddhism), sought refuge here for several months.

Zuri is six storeys high, its massive walls tapering outwards and dotted with narrow slits, through which soldiers could shoot arrows and fire cannon. Strategically located to defend Rinpung Dzong and the valley, the monastery is approached through a narrow bridge with a sheer drop on either side. Stone steps lead to the fort-temple's giant doors, made of massive curved logs of wood. From the beautiful temple on the fourth floor there is a panoramic view of the Paro Valley. The serene chapel on the third floor is dedicated to Guru Rimpoche, while the topmost floor, right under the roof, was used for storage and for throwing stone cannonballs down on attackers. A row of cypresses, believed to be around 400 years old, stand like sentinels in front of Zuri, adding to the evocative atmosphere of the place.

Back down in the valley, below the National Museum, is another unique temple, Dungtse Lhakhang, built—unusually for a temple—in the shape of a chorten. Dating back to 1421, Dungtse Lhakhang too was built to subdue a demoness, whose head it now pins down. This temple is literally chained down for it is believed that otherwise it will fly off to heaven. Inside Dungtse Lhakhang are the most remarkable collection of mural paintings, representing the deities of the Drukpa Kargyupa school of Buddhism, the official religion of Bhutan. These murals, their colours perfectly preserved because the interior is always dark, are believed to be the finest in all of Bhutan.

At its north-western end, the Paro Valley is dominated by the snow-white pyramid of Mt Chomolhari (7316 metres), which has aptly been likened to a giant ice cream cone, and the picturesque ruins of the seventeenth-century Drukgyel Dzong, which was destroyed in a devastating fire in 1951. Built to commemorate a famous victory over the Tibetans in 1644, the ruins are now an idyllic picnic spot, shaded by ancient cypress trees. Beside it is a giant water-driven prayer wheel, marking the route of the old mule track to Tibet. In the old days, this was a much-travelled trail, with traders from Bhutan taking rice to barter at Phari Dzong in Tibet, in exchange for salt and brick tea. In my childhood, my father regularly made the three-day journey to Phari in Tibet, passing by this prayer wheel, his pack mules laden with rice from our fields in Punakha.

A little beyond Drukgyel Dzong, I crossed the Mesi Zam suspension bridge, and continued my pilgrimage to temples hidden in the mountains above the valley. It was a beautiful spring morning, and my destination was Lhading, the Temple of the Flying Gods, a two-hour walk away. The path was lovely, much of it through forest, dotted with primulas, wild rose and spiraea bushes, anemones and wild strawberries. A short, steep climb at the end, and we were at Lhading, being greeted by Ap Kesang, the eighty-year-old caretaker and descendant of the founders of Lhading, who lives here with his son and daughter-in-law and grandchildren. Lhading is renowned for its remarkably beautiful, large and lifelike images, each with an exquisitely carved canopy over it. The statue of Chenrezig, the Bodhisattva of Compassion, is said to have spoken twice: '*Tsab ngagi tueb*' (I am the replacement), it said, when the bronze one that was here earlier was taken away to Tibet; and '*Zu de tsug*' (put me sideways), when it was brought here for installation in a standing position and could not fit through the low temple door.

Another treasure at Lhading is a huge book of scriptures with very heavy wooden covers, lavishly embossed with gold. It is believed that those who can lift this book will be cleansed of their sins, and those who cannot have sinned greatly. Fortunately for me I managed to lift it and place it against my forehead—the hand-weight training I had been doing had turned out to be good for my soul as well as for my muscles!

Over lunch, Ap Kesang told me the story of how Lhading was founded. A venerable Tibetan lama, Sakya Penchen, dispatched his disciple, an attendant lama and a donkey from Tibet to Bhutan. He told them that their mission was to find a lake, and the donkey knew where the lake was, so he should be treated kindly during the journey and not beaten. The donkey stopped at a clearing (later named Sa Bongku or the Land of the Donkey), where a group of vultures was hovering in the hill above. The disciple went to investigate, and found a lake. The blessed rice which Lama Sakya Penchen had sent with them was thrown into the lake, and the disciple prayed, 'If this is indeed the lake of destiny, let the water sink and sand rise.' When he awoke the next morning, the lake had disappeared and in its place was a bed of white sand. Lhading temple was built on that very spot. The vultures were the manifestations of the gods, revealing the site of the temple-to-be.

There is a tradition among the people of Paro to visit both Lhading and another temple, Tamchog, on a one-day pilgrimage, in the belief that this will wash away the sins accumulated over 300 rebirths. This time, I didn't go to Tamchog but to another temple, Jana, a four-hour walk away. It had started raining and I was tempted to give up the idea and return home, but then summoned up the resolve to 'Just Do It' (the Nike motto has often helped me in such moments!). The sight of an eighty-two-year-old woman, energetically harvesting her crop of foxtail millet in a village en route to Jana, spurred me on. As we skirted the hill and ascended through pine forests, the rain stopped and the sun shone. I stood on a ridge and far below, down in the valley, I could see through my binoculars village women in their colourful kiras busily planting paddy.

Now began the serious climb to the aptly named Jana Temple (Jana means 'in the mountains'). The ruins of several meditation huts stood some way below the temple—these meditation huts are where monks go to perform their solitary meditation, traditionally lasting three years, three months and three days. It is also not at all unusual for ordinary people to come to these huts for a few months or weeks, leaving behind their material concerns, living very simply and immersing themselves in the spiritual life for a while.

Jana belongs to the people of Tsento village which surrounds Drukgyel Dzong, and the Tsentops, who have traditionally guarded our northern frontiers, are reputed to be very fierce, robbing and sometimes killing those whom they think are intruders. Jana's endowment includes six acres of paddy land in Tsento village, the income from which is used to perform the death anniversary rituals of its founding lamas. On this day, about 400 people from Tsento come to Jana to pray, dance and celebrate, and spend the night camping in and around the temple. I too spent the night at Jana, in the temple on the second floor, from where there is a spectacular view of Drukgyel Dzong, and enjoyed the hospitality of Dophu the caretaker and his family, who claim descent from the founding lamas.

As I have mentioned earlier, all valleys and temples have their own protecting deities who were probably Bon deities earlier and were then assimilated into the Mahayana Buddhist pantheon. Protecting deities play an important part in people's lives—newborn babies are brought to them to be blessed and named, and when they grow up they turn to him for his blessings during examinations, weddings and other important occasions. At Jana, I met the parents of five babies who had come for the blessings of its Protecting Deity, Charee Tsen. The temple grounds have become a refuge for numerous goats, bulls and sheep, which were bought by devotees to save them from the butcher's knife and offered to the temple. Such acts of compassion for sentient beings are believed to earn one great merit.

I left Jana at six the next morning, and our next destination was Yum Tsho lake (Mother Lake). We walked through a landscape of stunning alpine beauty—the mountainside covered with flowering dwarf rhododendron bushes, streams of water running past rocks around which a profusion of flowers bloomed, forming a natural rock garden. Pheasants called from trees along our uphill path, and we even saw a pheasant's nest with three eggs in it—just like in the English storybooks we used to read at St Helen's convent. Herds of yaks grazed in green meadows. At one place, we walked through an alley of alpine magnolia bushes—white ones on one side and pink ones on the other. This was truly a garden of paradise. But alas, Yum Tsho lake was invisible, covered in mist, and so we climbed on for another hour to another lake, Dragay Pangtsho. This lake was an awesome sight, fed by eight different springs flowing down the mountain facing the lake. Dwarf rhododendron, pink, white and yellow, covered the banks of the lake. We had lunch in a tiny cave with a view of the entire lake, where I made a little fire for warmth.

I could have sat there for hours, but by now it was 1 p.m. and our next destination, Bumdra Monastery, where we were to spend the night, was seven hours away.

As we walked along the path to Bumdra, which is high above Taktsang, it was beginning to get dark. We had a steep and rocky mountain to climb before we reached the top of the Bumdra Pass, where dead children below the age of seven are brought for sky burial. Their bodies are left on a rock, to be consumed by the elements, so that their innocent young souls become a part of nature. By now my companion, Chime Pedoy, began to show signs of altitude sickness. Darkness had fallen, and our nerves and physical stamina were sorely tested—one false step on that narrow rocky path would have spelt disaster.

It was 11 p.m. before we finally reached Bumdra, and sixteen hours since we had left Jana that morning. Our guide had misjudged the distance—it would have been wiser to stop before dark and camp somewhere en route. It took the last reserves of my energy to climb the three flights of stairs to the main temple at Bumdra, where I prostrated three times at the altar before falling into a deep and dreamless sleep.

Bumdra means 'The Rock of a Hundred Thousand Footprints'. Legend has it that a hundred thousand *dakinis* (angels) descended here and left their footprints on a rock. It is also believed that in the eleventh century an emanation of Goddess Tara visited this place. The main temple at Bumdra is dedicated to Tara, whose beautiful image adorns the altar. The tiny footprints of the angels can be seen on a rock behind the altar. To the left of Bumdra are more tiny footprints—the angels are said to have flown back to heaven from this spot.

The next morning, we woke to a scene of pristine beauty—the temple is surrounded by meadows dotted with flowers. We were soon on our way, through forests of pine and juniper, to Ragoe Temple. On the way we met seventy-three-year-old Karchu, a carpenter and the caretaker of a small temple, together with his five-year-old grandson, Sonam Wangchuk. The little boy was a delight, lively and observant. Karchu told me he was the child of his daughter and a Japanese tourist, who had abandoned his daughter when she became pregnant. As compensation, he gave the family a TV and a tape recorder (for which they had no use) and Nu 40,000. The shock of this betrayal had caused his daughter to lose her mind, and the little boy was now, for all purposes, motherless.

As we neared Ragoe, I saw meditation huts perched above the temple. In the highest of these, my father's grandfather, Kuenga Gyeltshen (he who had built the face of the great Buddha statue in Paro Dzong, as well as our beautiful ancestral home, Kuengacholing), had meditated for three years. A steep descent from the narrow path led to the main temple of Ragoe. This path was renowned for the rocks on its sides, which bear amazing imprints. The Ragoe monks proudly pointed them out to us—a pair of serpents, the head and paw prints of a tiger, a goat, a vulture, Guru Rimpoche's footprint and the impression of his hat. These rocks also bear a striking likeness of what are believed to be 'angels' vaginas'—but when we came to these the monks suddenly fell silent in embarrassment!

In the main temple at Ragoe, the Guru Rimpoche image, flanked by his two consorts, took my breath away—his eyes sparkled with wisdom and compassion and he looked as if he was just about to speak. I sat for a while in the balcony of Ragoe, jutting out from the mountainside and supported on wooden poles. With a strange feeling of premonition I wondered what would happen if the whole structure were to collapse, for it felt rather precarious. And that is exactly what happened six weeks later, fortunately with no loss of life. Happily, Ragoe has now been rebuilt by Zepon Wangchuck, who almost miraculously restores our ancient monasteries and temples, while keeping intact their original character.

Having spent three unforgettable days in these sacred places hidden deep in the mountains around Paro, I now went back to Ugyen Pelri Palace, in the heart of Paro town, to spend the night, but resumed my pilgrimage the next day. I will write about just two of the five temples I visited over the next four days, though each one was a unique and sublime experience. Chumphu, a five-hour walk from the town, is famous throughout the Himalayan Buddhist world as the temple of Dorji Phagmo, a particularly powerful and revered goddess. Such is the awe in which she is held that she is rarely depicted in either paintings or statues. Chumphu not only had rare

images of Dorji Phagmo, but the largest of them is said to be
levitating, for a thread can be passed between her form and the base
on which she is seated. I offered my prayer beads in obeisance to this
extraordinary image of the goddess, and then sat down to enjoy the
delicious lunch brought by the head abbot of Paro. The other
treasures of Chumphu include an ancient Buddha seated on a lotus,
and a phurpa (ritual dagger) made by Desi Tenzin Rabgye.

Chumphu is also famous as one of the *beyul*s or Hidden Lands
designated by Guru Rimpoche—havens of extraordinary peace and
beauty, which I have written about in some detail in the next
chapter. Lush greenery surrounds Chumphu, and there is a little lake
above the temple. The bamboo growing around the lake is what we
call the sacred *tsare yuemo*, said to be a long-life talisman. We took
some of these bamboo shoots with us as we made our way down
from Chumphu, through the shade of a forest, following the course
of the frothing, turbulent river. The spell of this day was, alas,
broken by the sight of an ancient chorten which had been robbed,
its roof smashed in by robbers who wanted to steal the rare agates,
which we call zee, and other valuable relics, blessed and interred
here centuries ago. The zees fetch a huge price in countries such as
Taiwan. The robbing of relics from these ancient chortens is a
relatively new phenomenon—I wonder what kind of greed can make
anyone commit the sin of robbing and desecrating these symbols of
pure and humble devotion.

Of all the temples in the Paro Valley, perhaps the most spectacular
location is that of Dongkarla. If you fly into Paro this is the only
temple that you see if you look up, well above the level at which the
plane is flying. Dongkarla covers the crest of a high hill, and has a
breathtaking 360-degree view of the valleys and peaks around. Time
seemed to have stood still at Dongkarla—as we came round the last
bend in the path, we saw the winter snow lying still unmelted. The
silence was broken only by the call of partridge and pheasant.
Dongkarla too has a very beautiful Guru Rimpoche statue, with a
legend attached to it—the chaplain told us that when the statue was
about to be taken back to the temple of its origin, nobody could lift
it, and then it spoke and declared that it would stay here.

It was at Dongkarla that I saw one of the most curious relics I have ever seen in a temple. It was a well-preserved human hand, cut off at the wrist, hanging in the temple of the protecting deity. This was said to be the hand of a thief who had come to steal the antique brass cauldron used for auspicious ceremonies. But as soon as he touched the cauldron, his hand got stuck to it, and he had no option but to cut it off, in order to escape—a cautionary tale that the chorten robbers would do well to heed!

CHAPTER 10

HIDDEN PARADISE

'The Last Shangri La' is a phrase much used (and overused) in tourist brochures about Bhutan. Most Bhutanese, however, have no idea what Shangri La means—the word was invented by James Hilton in his book *Lost Horizon*, to describe a hidden paradise somewhere in the Himalayas. What Hilton didn't invent is the fact that these hidden paradises do exist. But we have another name for them—we call them beyuls. According to our tradition, beyuls are places chosen by Guru Padmasambhava, scattered throughout the Himalayan region, which will remain havens of tranquillity in times of turmoil and violence, providing a safe refuge for people, and for their religion and culture. Several of Guru Padmasambhava's chosen beyuls are in Bhutan and, not surprisingly, they are places that are well off the beaten track.

My travels on foot throughout Bhutan have taken me to more than one beyul. They are indeed idyllic places, of great serenity and beauty. But unlike James Hilton's Shangri La, where no one ever grows old, the beyuls I have been to certainly have their share of old people, who have experienced the sorrows and burdens of human existence. Nevertheless there is an intangible quality about beyuls that sets them apart from other beautiful places—people who live there seem to have an instinctive understanding of the true art of living, a healthy detachment from purely material pursuits, an ability to recognize and enjoy the gifts of nature, and the wisdom to accept and face life's vicissitudes.

My first experience of a beyul was in February 2000, when I set off on the first of my walking tours of Bhutan, to acquaint myself at first-hand with people who live in some of the most inaccessible parts of the country. I chose to begin with what is traditionally known as the Kheng region in central Bhutan, covering the districts of Zhemgang and Mongar. This is a densely forested region with a population of 26,000, who live scattered in a succession of narrow valleys enclosed by steep slopes. There are hardly any motor roads here. There is scarcely any flat land. Because of this difficult terrain, the Khengpas literally fight an uphill battle to make their living from agriculture and animal husbandry. Swidden agriculture—more commonly known as the slash-and-burn method of cultivation, where a piece of forest land is cleared by burning, cultivated for a while and then left fallow to renew itself—is particularly prevalent in Kheng. Though frowned upon by conservationists today, it seems the people of Kheng know how to manage this practice—forest cover in Zhemgang is 86 per cent, well over the national average of 72 per cent.

With the lack of roads and the steep barriers between valleys, village communities in Kheng tend to be very self-contained, cut off not just from the outside world but from each other. One of the consequences of this isolation is that they are quite unaware of what is happening in other parts of Bhutan, and one of the aims of our tour was to introduce new techniques of agriculture and land use that would improve yields, increase incomes and add some variety to their diet. District officials who had tried to do so in the past had found the Khengpas rather resistant to change. Another consequence of the isolation of Kheng villages is the survival of ancient shamanistic rites and Bon rituals that have died out elsewhere in the country.

My walking route would take in some of the most remote villages of Zhemgang district, from where I would walk over the Nuemola Pass into Mongar district, and eventually end my tour at

Kurichu in eastern Bhutan. It would mean fourteen days of hard walking, with no possibility of jumping into a car en route in case my stamina gave out. My endurance training was limited to sessions on an exercise bike, but with the insouciance born of ignorance, I decided I could do it. I didn't then fully realize that walking through Kheng would entail not pleasant ambles through idyllic rural landscapes, but an endless series of gruelling ascents and descents, the former agonizing for the lungs, calves and thighs, and the latter killing for the knees and toes.

Laden with packets of seeds, new agricultural tools, essential medicines and clothes to distribute along the way, my companions and I started the tour of Kheng where the motor road ends, at Praleng. We walked at a brisk pace, each trying to impress the other on this first day, taking a brief stop for lunch at Kamjong village, where the villagers were busy tilling their maize fields. The first day's walk was a kind of baptism by fire—by the time we reached camp at Dunmang village (not to be confused with Dunmang hot springs) that evening, we had walked for thirteen hours. Though I would have given anything to crawl straight into bed that evening, I steeled myself to meet the twenty-seven households of the village. I had brought spades, sets of clothing for the oldest villagers, and packets of seeds for them. With the blunt good humour which I was to encounter throughout Kheng, the villagers of Dunmang told me that they found broccoli and carrots unpalatable, and preferred to feed it to their pigs, though the district agriculture office had tried hard to persuade them to grow new kinds of vegetables. The maize storage containers we were trying to introduce, to protect their maize from vermin, were also greeted with some consternation. It was their practice, some of the villagers admitted, to convert much of their maize to alcohol, as that way the worms and rats wouldn't get it. But with these new pest-proof containers, they no longer had an excuse to brew alcohol! After this salutary lesson in the pitfalls of being a do-gooder, I collapsed with aching limbs and blisters on my heels. How would I last out the thirteen days ahead?

Early the next morning, our walking trail took us on an interminable descent down to the Chamkarchhu river, at the end of which I had huge blisters on my toes to join those on my heels from the day before. We crossed a suspension bridge across the river before beginning an almost vertical ascent up to the village of Digala. Midway through I found my feet could not carry me any further—I gave in and rode the rest of the way. At Digala, where I spent the night, I met a shaman from the area in his fearsome regalia of necklaces made of claws and animal skulls, who drummed and danced at a frenetic pace before going into a trance and then falling into a swoon. This was the first of many Bon rituals I was to witness during this tour. That night I was in agony. I took paracetamol, thought of the twelve days of walking ahead, and wished a helicopter would come and whisk me away.

A good night's sleep did wonders for my morale and, fortunately, the next day's walk, to the delightful village of Langdurbi, was not too taxing. Here, as in most of the villages I would see on this tour, the houses were mostly two-storeyed, solidly built of stone and rubble, and the roofs thatched with banana leaves. Inside, seed maize cobs hung from the ceiling, tall hollow bamboo containers of home-distilled ara stood fermenting, and everywhere there was evidence of the Khengpas' skill in weaving the cane that grows so abundantly in their forests—baskets, saddlebags, mats, hats, wicker chests, winnowers and sieves. Some of the baskets were ingeniously lined with rubber from the trees that grow wild here, so that they could be used for carrying liquids as well. Outside the houses were great millstones for grinding corn. I tried my hand at this but produced just a handful of cornmeal after an hour's effort.

My campsite at Langdurbi was a grassy hollow where there was once a lake. Our sleeping shelters were enchanting, constructed out of branches and foliage, roofed with banana leaves, with scarlet rhododendrons threaded through the leaves. Similar shelters, straight out of a fairy tale, were built for us in almost every village on this tour.

I spent two nights at Langdurbi, meeting people from its forty-seven households, and witnessed more shamanistic dances and rituals. Here the shaman sat on a bed of stinging nettles, drumming and chanting as he flagellated himself with a bunch of nettles on his neck, shoulders and legs. Then followed a ritual called Kharpo, in honour of a Bon deity, conducted by a man in white turban and gho. The ritual took place around an altar where the main object was a huge wooden phallus, its crown painted red, placed on banana leaves. In a sonorous voice the man in white invoked the deities from the thirteen realms and sought their blessings, as offerings of ara and water were placed on the altar. Six men joined him and chanted in chorus as they went round and round the altar. It was a hypnotic scene.

The next stage of my journey began with a truly terrifying walk—there is an infamous precipice between Langdurbi and the next village, Khomshar, and we inched our way along the footpath, because it was both narrow and slippery with loose gravel. Far down below was the roaring river. I drew my breath and, I think, only let it out once all of us, including the pack mules, were safely across the precipice. With a light heart we now walked through the villages of Pachar, Zilingbi and Dunglabi. Along the way, we saw imprints of Guru Padmasambhava's foot and back on a rock—we were approaching one of his chosen hidden havens, the beyul of Khomshar, so effectively sealed off from the outside world by that forbidding precipice.

After negotiating a sharp bend, Khomshar came into view. The village has a magnificent site, covering a ridge at the top of a mountain, and cascading down the sleep slopes. The upper slopes have wheat and millet fields, with terraced rice fields lower down the mountainside. At Khomshar, as at Langdurbi, the main meeting place in the village is a grassy hollow where there was once a lake. I sank down on the soft grass and listened as the villagers proudly read out from their ancient scriptures the description of Khomshar as one of Guru Padmasambhava's beyuls. They pointed out more signs of the Guru's blessings—a rock with a deep cavity in it, with a little stone chorten inside it, said to have been naturally formed. Below the dry lake bed where we were sitting was, I was told, an ancient one-room temple with the Guru's foot- and handprints.

In these idyllic surroundings, I ate a memorably delicious lunch prepared by the villagers of Khomshar. First I had a refreshing soup made with wild yam and seasoned with the fragrant wild pepper (zanthozylum) that grows here, served in a cup made of hollowed bamboo. Then came dishes made of tender fiddlehead ferns, cane and bamboo shoots, banana cobs, amaranthus seeds, buckwheat pancakes, river weeds and a variety of mushrooms—all these harvested from the forest and the river, and all part of the staple diet in Khomshar and the other villages I had walked through. These gifts of nature, which are available in abundance in this area, require no labour to cultivate, and provide delicious and nutritious food for the people of Khomshar—no wonder this place is regarded as close to heaven.

At Khomshar, too, I witnessed religious rites that the village had observed for many centuries. An altar was set up outdoors, again with a wooden phallus as its centerpiece. The blessings of the deities that are worshipped in the village were invoked through ceremonies known as Kuenlahari, Gophu and Sacram. Once again the gods were summoned from their thirteen realms with the chanting of prayers and drumming, and then bid a respectful farewell at the end of the invocation ceremony. Then followed a highly acrobatic dance by the men of the village, in which their hands were tied behind their backs. Each man then bent down to pick up a brimming cup of ara with his lips, without spilling a drop. At the end of this spectacular performance the women and children of Khomshar got up and joined in the dance, and as though under a spell, I too found myself in the circle of dancers.

During lunch earlier in the day, a feisty, bright-eyed village elder had caught my eye. Meme (grandpa) Penjor told me that as a young man he had been a cattle herdsman for the second king. And now, at the age of eighty-nine, he laughingly declared, he was preparing to meet his other king, Chogegyalpo, the Lord of Judgement and Death. Meme Penjor's wife had become a nun twenty years earlier, and moved to Thimphu, from where she occasionally sent him parcels of powdered milk. Because of the lack of roads and the hardships of travel in this difficult terrain, most people in Khomshar and other villages in the interior of Kheng have never been further than their neighbourhood, growing up, marrying, raising their children and dying in the place where they were born. Meme Penjor and his wife were exceptions. In his youth, he said, he had journeyed far out of the village, taking the king's herds of cattle to their winter and summer grazing grounds, and selling butter and cheese in Bumthang and Kuenga Rabden. Yet his travels had only convinced him there was no place on earth more beautiful than Khomshar, and no way of life more harmonious. He was happy to spend his last years here, he said, finding joy in watching his grandchildren grow. Moved by his proud and independent spirit, which never admitted to loneliness or want, I decided on the spur of the moment to 'adopt' him and provide him an annual stipend that would ensure he never had to ask anyone for money to take care of his needs. Meme Penjor was the first adoptee of the Tarayana Foundation, which I set up to take care of especially vulnerable people.

Before leaving this real-life Shangri La, the beyul of Khomshar, I gave a spade to each of the 110 households of the village. Each spade weighed 1.4 kilos, and lifting and handing it over 110 times was quite a work-out—I could almost see my biceps grow! Perhaps now I would succeed in grinding corn on the *rangtha* grindstone, as the Kheng women seemed to do so effortlessly.

From Khomshar our route led downhill to the river and then steeply uphill again to the Bardo, a village with sixty-seven households. Once again I 'cheated' and rode uphill, the better to admire the beautiful rhododendron forests along the way, now in full bloom. The mountainsides were a blaze of colour—in shades of scarlet, white and mauve. From Bardo it was another steep descent—this time on foot, not on horseback. I remembered a saying from my childhood, taught to us by grandfather Ashang Samdu: 'A horse that cannot carry its master uphill is no horse,' he would say during those long horseback journeys to school in India, 'and a master who rides his horse downhill is no master.' Then began the steepest uphill climb of this journey, up to the Nuemola Pass, which would lead us into Mongar district. There was no question of riding up—the track was slippery, like a polished earthen slide, because for centuries the villagers of Kheng have been harvesting bamboo from the Nuemola forests, and sliding it down this track. Nuemola bamboo is famous for being exceptionally flexible and durable, and in the olden days was much in demand by the aristocracy of Bhutan for making their arrows and quill pens.

The pass was covered in snow and mist and we slowly negotiated our way down to Wama village in Mongar district. Here I was greeted by the villagers with a whole roasted piglet and countless hollow bamboo containers full of home-brewed ara—enough to last me a couple of years, even if I drank it every day. It would be unforgivably rude to spurn these generous gifts, so I suggested an impromptu community feast, during which the piglet and the ara were consumed in no time. While at Wama, where I spent the night, I offered to help a family grind their daily corn on their grindstone. The maize is fed through a hole in the top slab, which has a wooden handle that is used to rotate the stone to grind the corn. My attempts produced no more than a spoonful, but they did provide the village considerable amusement.

The next morning, en route to the next village, Silambi, I met a South Indian engineer, G. Kurukesu, engaged in constructing a suspension bridge over the Sherigangchhu river. He told me he had built twenty-eight bridges in Bhutan so far. I marvelled at this man who had spent so many years doing the most difficult and dangerous work in the remotest parts of Bhutan, so far away from the comforts and modern conveniences of his home. He seemed very happy with his lot—perhaps he had discovered his own beyul in Bhutan.

Silambi is renowned throughout Bhutan for its *bangchus*—the round, multicoloured lidded containers made of thin strips of cane, which can be found in every Bhutanese home. We had a set of them at home in Nobgang, in which my father and grandfather would carry their lunch to the fields, and my mother would store her weaving yarns. And no Bhutanese sets out on a journey without a bangchu full of toasted corn or rice to provide instant energy. Sir John Claude White, writing in 1914, was struck by their fine craftsmanship: 'They are made in two circular pieces, rounded top and bottom, and the two pieces fit so closely and well that they can be used to carry water, [though] they are principally used to carry cooked rice and food.'

I watched a housewife in Silambi split, dye and weave the cane into intricate patterns, and thought how the skill of women in this tiny, remote village brought colour and beauty to households all over the country.

Over the next four days, my tour took me to the villages of Nagor, Dagsa, Bambangla and Resa, each of which warmed my heart with their hospitality, and their attachment to their wild and beautiful land, despite all the hardships it entailed. By now, I had begun to find my uphill legs and my downhill legs, and it was no longer so daunting to face those unrelenting series of ascents and descents. Almost every village I visited on this trip wanted a motorable road to reach closer to them, but not a single one wanted to relocate to more accessible and fertile areas in southern Bhutan.

Throughout the tour, I came across an extraordinarily large number of young unmarried mothers, some barely into their teens, duped by the false promises of men who had passed through their villages and were never seen again. One anaemic little boy I met in Bambangla told me that his father was a doctor in Thimphu. I racked my brains, wondering which doctor in Thimphu had a little son in remote Bambangla. Later I was told that in these parts, 'doctor in Thimphu' is the usual euphemism used by unmarried mothers and their children, for the men who have abandoned them.

During the tour, I also found an unusually large number of people with harelip. This congenital deformity not only affected their speech and food consumption, but also their self-esteem. The high occurrence of harelip in this area is probably a result of consanguinity in these self-contained and isolated communities, where there has been much intermarriage over the generations. In Nagor village alone, I found twelve people with this disability, among them a fifty-six-year-old man who solemnly declared that if his face could be rebuilt, many women would fall in love with him. A ripple of laughter broke out among the villagers.

The last village I visited was Resa, from where we crossed a bridge over the Kurichhu river, walked through a stretch of forest, and there ahead of us was the road, with cars waiting. My first instinct was to turn around and retreat back into the world in which I had just spent fourteen unforgettable days.

Looking back on this journey now, I realize that it marked a turning point in my life. It taught me how best to involve myself in a small but hands-on and intimate way with the lives of our people. It opened my eyes to the challenge—and importance—of finding the right balance between bringing the benefits of development to people in remote communities without destroying their unique cultures. And it was on this journey that I decided to start the Tarayana Foundation, which has, until now, 'adopted' 379 people of all ages—from ninety-year-olds to teenagers and infants—with special needs and vulnerabilities. Our foundation now takes care of their food, social security and medical needs. We have started special schemes to help unmarried mothers and their children. And we have been able to organize two rounds of surgery for people with harelip or cleft palates. The before-and-after pictures tell what a transformation the surgery has wrought in their lives.

And finally, this arduous two-week tour gave me the courage to undertake many more such journeys on foot into remote corners of the country. For me, these have all been great voyages of discovery.

CHAPTER 11

LA YA!

Winter in the Punakha Valley is heralded every year by the arrival of the Layaps, with their arresting faces and unusual dress. Hailing from the remote northern region of Laya, they trek down from their highland home to the warmer valleys, laden with meat, rich yellow butter and cheese made from yak's milk, sacks of fragrant alpine herbs which are used to make the best kind of incense, as well as medicinal plants. These they barter in Punakha for rice, chillies, salt, cloth and oil. The Layaps have been a familiar sight right from my childhood, milling around Punakha Dzong from November to February, or soaking in the hot springs at Gasa where we used to go with my grandparents every year. I found the women especially intriguing, with their long hair, pointed cane hats ornamented with pearls and beads, and black wool dress, against which their heavy silver jewellery, studded with large corals and turquoise, stood out to stunning effect.

There is a curious legend about the origin of the Layaps and their strange way of dressing. It is said that they originally lived in southern Tibet, in a region that was suddenly struck by a series of disasters. Clearly, a curse had fallen on the region, but how was it to be got rid of? The local practice for ending a spell of misfortune was to perform a voodoo-like ritual, by making doll-sized figures of clay or dough, dress them in black costumes and make them scapegoats for the misfortune. They were then symbolically loaded with the curses and bad luck and cast out of the area. But in this case, so powerful was the curse that it was felt human scapegoats had to be found, and the choice fell on the entire population of a particular village. These unfortunate villagers were made to wear a strange black costume and pointed hat, similar to those put on the dummy figures, and banished en masse, taking away with them the ill luck that had dogged the region. The hapless villagers wandered homeless for several days until they stumbled upon a beautiful valley, with the majestic Mount Masagang (7144 metres) towering over it. 'La Ya!!' they exclaimed in wonder and admiration, and that is what they decided to name their new home. They continued wearing their strange costume because, in the end, it had brought them good luck.

In October 2001, when I accompanied my mother to the Gasa hot springs, I decided to go on to Laya, which is a two-day walk from Gasa, and then continue on to Lingzhi. This stretch of the country is the home of the blue sheep and the blue poppy, the rare snow leopard and the takin (more about the takin later). Above all, it is prime yak country. The Lingzhi–Laya route is a favourite one with foreign trekkers, with its magnificent alpine landscapes ringed by several peaks above 7000 metres. I was going to do the trek in the reverse direction from that which the tourists take, crossing four high passes en route. For me, this was a long-awaited opportunity to meet the Layaps and other yak-herding communities in their own environment, and learn about their unique culture and semi-nomadic way of life.

Feeling blithe and full of energy after spending a day soaking in the Gasa hot springs, I had a spring in my step as I made the steep climb up from the springs to the fairytale-like Gasa Dzong, from where the trail to Laya begins. It was a beautiful, sunny day, and the first day's walk was not too strenuous. We spent the night comfortably in a community hut at Koina, by the banks of a stream. With its central common room warmed by a hearth, this hut is where the Layaps usually spend the night on their way down to Gasa and Punakha.

The next day's walk was even lovelier, the air crystal clear and fragrant, the trees displaying every shade of autumn colour. Our trail, which followed the course of a river, was gentle enough so that we could talk without panting as we walked. The hours passed easily, until I came across a blind and pregnant young widow called Wangmo, sitting under a tree. Her six-year-old son acted as her guide. Wangmo had a tragic story to tell—she no longer felt welcome in her in-laws' house after her husband's death, and being a proud woman decided not to put up with their insults and humiliation any longer. She had rigged up a makeshift shelter under the tree, where she would await the birth of her baby. I thought to myself, not for the first time, that human beings can be more cruel than any other species. The Tarayana Foundation 'adopted' Wangmo. We were able to give her a home before her baby was born three months later, and a monthly stipend.

By late afternoon we were on the outskirts of Laya, at 3800 metres, where our arrival was preceded by near disaster. Just a few minutes before we entered the valley, we stopped to watch two enormous yaks, their horns locked in battle on a steep slope above our path. All of a sudden, the defeated yak charged down the slope at great speed towards us. I fled out of his path with just seconds to spare. And minutes later, heart still racing, I entered the ceremonial gateway to Laya which had been erected to welcome our party. It was an enchanting scene that lay before us—a broad plateau watched over by the snow peaks of Mount Masagang, dotted with handsome stone houses and grazing yaks, with hundreds of prayer flags fluttering in the breeze, and the haunting song of a herder floating over the valley as he rounded up his animals.

Dusk had already fallen, the campfire was lit in the centre of the village, and all the Layaps gathered round it to entertain us. In the glow of the firelight, the women performed their traditional dance, and the men sang in their full-throated voices. There was one particularly plaintive song, in which a male yak who is too old to carry loads pleads with his owner not to kill him at the annual culling, but to let him end his days peacefully in Laya's flower-filled pastures. After the entertainment, the Layap women all took off their pointed cane hats and threw them down in a heap, in their traditional gesture of respect for visitors. Afterwards I was intrigued to see how each woman unerringly identified her own hat, since to me they looked absolutely identical. It was late at night when the gathering broke up and I went to bed.

Laya is the most populous of the four gewogs or counties in Gasa district. It has 138 households, a community school, a basic health unit, and a newly built agriculture centre, where I was lodged. The yak is central to the lives of the Layaps, the main source of their food, clothing as well as shelter. In spring and summer, the Layaps leave their homes in the valley and migrate with their yaks to higher pastures, where they live in black yak-hair tents made from wool that they weave themselves. These tents are waterproof, and so strong that they last for decades. At the peak of winter, the Layaps are again on the move, bringing their prized yak meat, butter and herbs to sell or barter in the lower valleys. Another good source of income for them is as porters—they are famous for their stamina, and even the women carry fifty-kilo loads. The growing popularity of the Lingzhi–Laya trail with foreign trekkers has brought a welcome new source of income and employment for the Layaps, who serve as their guides and porters.

The Layap women's black wool ankle-length skirt (called the *zoom*) and jacket (called *khenja*) is woven from yak hair—the pattern is simple, with just some vertical stripes. Their fashion statement is made through their shoulder-length hair and a profusion of silver jewellery, which they even wear on their backs—apart from necklaces and bracelets they also sport charming little silver spoons, which probably come in handy on their travels. Unlike elsewhere in Bhutan where weaving is strictly women's work, in Laya the men also participate—it is they who spin the yak hair into thread, using a drop spindle. Apart from clothes and tents, yak hair is also used to make very durable ropes and sacks, and the warmest blankets.

There is a house in Laya which is famous in Bhutanese history, and that was where I made my first visit the next morning. When Zhabdrung Ngawang Namgyel, the founder of the Bhutanese state, fled to Bhutan from Tibet in 1616, the first place in which he was given shelter was this house in Laya. In 1606, the Zhabdrung had been enthroned as the eighteenth Prince-Abbot of Ralung Monastery in Tibet, and head of the Drukpa Kargyupa sect of Buddhism. But there was another claimant to the throne of Ralung, who was supported by the powerful ruler of Tsang province. Facing constant harassment and hearing reports that the Tsang ruler intended to attack Ralung and kill him, the Zhabdrung decided to leave for Bhutan. He had many followers in Bhutan, where his ancestors had built several monasteries. Among his staunchest supporters was the revered Obtsho Lama of Gasa, who urged him to come to Bhutan. Thus, in 1616, at the age of twenty-two, the Zhabdrung and his entourage crossed the frontier and arrived in Laya, where the Obtsho Lama was waiting to greet him.

The house belongs to the family of the hereditary gups or headmen of Laya, and they are proud custodians of the gifts the Zhabdrung gave their ancestors nearly 400 years ago—a three-sided turquoise of the clearest blue colour and a magnificent copper cauldron. This house had bags of rice stacked all the way up to the ceiling—a prime status symbol in Laya where they signified affluence and food security, and never mind if the rice was too old to be of any nutritional value!

The next house I visited was that of Aum Rinchen, a handsome widow of fifty-five, who had two beautiful little grandchildren. Her widowed thirty-four-year-old son, Tenzin, lived with her—tragically, his young wife had thrown herself into the river seven years earlier, and he had decided not to remarry. Tenzin, who owned forty-two yaks (including twelve riding yaks) and five horses, was a man of average wealth in Laya—the richest own herds of over 300. I learned from him that a fully grown female yak weighs around 300 kilos, and a bull yak around 500 kilos (just as well I managed to get out of the way of the charging bull!). And yet, despite their bulk they are extremely sure-footed animals, able to climb almost vertical slopes, walk through deep snow and negotiate the narrow spaces between rocks with incongruously dainty steps!

My next stop was the poorest household in the village—single-storey, made of wood and stone, displaying a mere seven bags of rice. The owner was an unmarried woman. I discovered that, as in Kheng, there are an unusually large number of children born out of wedlock to teenage mothers in Laya—the result of brief encounters with men passing through. There is no stigma attached to these children, but life is tough for their mothers, who have to struggle alone to make a living in an environment that demands hard physical labour. Just handling the yaks requires tremendous muscle power.

Marriage is a simple affair in Laya, entered into without any formal ceremony or rites. The custom is that if a young man spends the night with a girl and then stays on to have breakfast with her family, it is understood that he is now married to her. On the other hand, if he sneaks out like a thief in the night, without meeting any of the girl's family, then it is clear that he has no intention of making a lasting commitment.

The custom of polyandry is also prevalent in Laya, with one woman married to several brothers. I called on one such woman, the forty-three-year-old Yanki, who is married to four brothers. Tall and fair, with large eyes, a generous smile, beautiful jewellery and wavy hair liberally greased with mustard oil, Yanki was the veritable queen of Laya. Her large double-storeyed house boasted an impressive display of carpets, quilts, sacks of dried fish and, of course, dozens of bags of rice, all stacked up against the wall. She had four children, she told me, but refused to divulge who the father of each child was. 'They are *all* the fathers of *all* my children,' she told me, adding that she had no favourite husband. Her petite mother-in-law listened approvingly. She did eventually reveal that Husband Number Four, Lhabab Sethup, nine years younger than her, was the father of her young school-going child. The eldest was the one who delegated responsibilities to his younger brothers. There was a relaxed, happy atmosphere in that household, and Yanki had clearly mastered the art of keeping all her husbands happy. With four husbands, there were plenty of hands to look after the family's fortunes, which include a flourishing shop and, of course, a large herd of yaks.

The wealthiest household in Laya belongs to a former National Assembly member, who displayed his wealth in the usual way—in his case there were so many bags of rice, they literally shored up his house. His wife brought out her best jewels to show me—three strands of large red corals, a splendid turquoise and rare zees. Their unmarried daughter has two children from different fathers but, in contrast to the unmarried mother I had met earlier, her doting parents see to it that she and her children want for nothing.

The Laya women are renowned for their looks, and there was one famous beauty whose face adorned all our calendars and tourism brochures some years ago. When I met her, she was thirty-seven, the mother of eight children and, though the bloom of youth had faded, still lovely. I also met the new poster girl, eighteen-year-old Pey Dechen, who with her chiselled features, pink cheeks and dazzling smile will doubtless go on to become an icon of Layap beauty.

High above the village is the temple, with seventeen monks studying under a lama. The ceremonies and rituals they conduct include a special one to propitiate the local mountain deity, Gorap Chardo. The Layaps select their finest yaks, adorn them with beautifully woven coloured tassels and saddles, and then symbolically offer them to the deity. These consecrated yaks, easy to spot in all their finery, are truly magnificent specimens. At the temple, we tasted a rich local delicacy called *chugo margo*—hard yak cheese cooked in butter and sugar—which is a must at the annual community feast that follows the yak-consecration ceremony.

On my last evening in Laya, the community once again gathered round the campfire, and we talked late into the night. I learned about the very particular pleasures and perils of yak-herding as a livelihood. The Layaps clearly love their yaks and develop a rapport with each of their animals; each yak is given a name, and spoken to lovingly. Yaks are high-maintenance animals. A herdsmen spends up to 100 working days a year just collecting grass for making hay for the yaks. Yaks are shy animals and scare easily, and when they're scared they run away—the herders spend a lot of their time searching for animals who have gone astray. Yaks are also picky eaters. They don't like grazing in forests or eating shrubs; they prefer open meadows and plants that grow on the meadow floor. The beautiful saussurea flower species are particular favourites and lead to improved milk yields. The herders closely watch for signs from nature before they decide on their grazing schedules. When the primulas begin to flower in spring, it is time to move to the higher pasture grounds, and when the barley crop is harvested in the valley it is time to descend to lower altitudes. Yaks are excellent draught and pack animals, able to plough three times the amount of ground as oxen can in the same time, and carry average loads of eighty kilos in their saddlebags.

A major lament of the Layaps is the high mortality among yak calves—they told me they lose 20 per cent of their calves due to wild animal attacks, poor nutrition in the severe winter months, gid disease (caused by tapeworm larvae in the brain) and falls from cliffs or narrow mountain paths. This figure goes up to 50 per cent in Lunana, as I was to find out when I went there. Another complaint I heard from the Layaps was about the deterioration of their grazing grounds, mainly because of the growing herds of blue sheep and marmots—while the blue sheep are voracious consumers of pasture grass, the marmots' burrows and tunnels cause erosion on the slopes and deep hollow pits beneath the ground, into which the unsuspecting yaks often fall.

The culling of male yaks takes place in October and November, and yak meat is much sought after all over Bhutan. Lean and tender, with the flavour of alpine plants, it is more delicious than the best beef fillet, and is particularly delicious when it is air dried and eaten with a fiery chilli paste. The largest yaks, I was told, are found in Lingzhi, which I would head towards the next morning.

I left Laya riding a magnificent chocolate-coloured yak called Galey—a gift for me from the widower Tenzin. Galey was twelve years old, with a white forehead, and too old to be of any use as a breed bull or a draught animal. But this was a gift I could not keep—Galey would not survive at the altitude of Thimphu. I left money for his upkeep and, remembering the haunting song I had heard on my first evening in Laya, I made Tenzin promise me that he would not have Galey slaughtered, but would let him end his days grazing peacefully.

Our campsite that night was the beautiful valley of Limethang (also known locally as Memthang), with a sparkling stream running through it, and a lake. It was the last two weeks of the trekking season, and we shared the campsite with four groups of tourists. All of us were entertained that evening around the campfire by the songs and dances of two cheeky little teenaged Laya girls who had followed us. The next morning, I said goodbye to Tenzin and the yak Galey, and walked on towards our first high pass, the Shinjila, at 5030 metres. En route, the magnificent mountain Gangchen Ta revealed itself as the clouds parted briefly. It was a much-awaited rendezvous with the mountain—I had grown up looking at it from my village, Nobgang, and now here it was, right in front of me! At Zapokto, just before we began the ascent of the pass, we sat down for tea, and the Laya porters got up to perform nine lively dances. Energized by their strong voices and swift movements, we made the hard climb over the Shinjila Pass in three hours and fifteen minutes, and arrived at the Jigme Dorji National Park, named after the third king of Bhutan.

The park, covering an area of 4329 square kilometres, encompasses the northern portions of Punakha, Thimphu and Paro districts, and is incredibly rich in rare Himalayan flora and fauna. The red panda, the musk deer, the monal pheasant with its iridescent feathers, the rare and elusive snow leopard, and the curious-looking takin, the national animal of Bhutan, can all be found here. There is a Bhutanese legend about the origin of the takin—after God had finished creating all the different creatures on earth, he had an odd assortment of leftovers. And so he made the takin, with the head of a goat, the nose of a moose, the body of a cow and the ears of a horse. This lumbering animal, about the size of a cow, golden brown in colour, has been scientifically classified as a goat-antelope. Females weigh between 200 to 500 kilos and males between 400 to 1000 kilos. The manager of the Jigme Dorji National Park, who is a takin expert, led us to a saltlick where a group of takins had gathered. I learned that there are about 180 takins in the Jigme Dorji National Park, which provides them an ideal habitat with its saltlicks, clean water and abundant grass. The takin also eats the poisonous flowers of the high-altitude aconite plant without any ill effects, and in Bhutanese traditional medicine its meat used to be greatly prized— a dish of takin was reputed to be able to revive a near-dead person. Today, of course, hunting or killing the takin, of which there are only an estimated 500 in Bhutan, is strictly forbidden.

Walking upstream from the saltlick, we stopped for cheese at a yak herder's black tent, guarded by his enormous mastiff. These enormous shaggy dogs, the size of a small donkey, have been known to fight off leopards—they are excellent as watchdogs and at rounding up animals. A short while after that we came upon the impressive ruins of an old dzong on a hill, with the scattered stones of what must have been a village at the base of the hill. We had reached our campsite at Tsarijathang. The ruined dzong had thick stone walls that displayed a high standard of masonry. I escaped to spend a few quiet moments by myself in the tiny temple of the ruined fort, away from the porters and travelling companions, and mused about the long-ago king and queen who must have lived in this romantic frontier fort and ruled over their nomadic subjects. Looking down from my hilltop perch I saw herds of takins and blue sheep grazing. The blue sheep (*Pseudonis nayaur*)—the favourite food of the snow leopard—actually has a slate grey coat that appears bluish in winter.

That evening, all the yak herders scattered at different encampments in the region gathered at Tsarijathang, bearing gifts of milk, butter and cheese. It was a rare opportunity for all of them to get together and there was much animated discussion about breed bulls, animals for sale, the current year's prices for yak meat and butter and so on. The evening ended, as always, with songs. The next morning, as I toiled up the Jarila Pass, I met a group of tourists whose impressive entourage included thirty-nine yaks, nine attendants including a cook, and eight gas cylinders being carried by the yaks, for wood is scarce in these parts and is not allowed to be used for cooking or heating water for trekkers. I joked with the cook to be sure to feed his party yak milk and yogurt—for those not used to it, yak milk, with its rich fat content, causes immediate diarrhoea!

The last of the autumn flowers made a brilliant blaze of colour all along our trail—yellow saxifrage, scarlet sedum, pink bistorta, star-shaped white edelweiss, deep blue gentian, tall stalks of purple aconite and phlomis, and as we descended, pink and white berries hanging from sorbus bushes. When our campsite at Jasipasang Valley came into view from a hilltop I spotted two identical little tarns next to each other, shaped like a pair of dark glasses in the upturned 1960s style. Another curiosity was a large stone near our tent with round eyes, broad nose and wide mouth—an object that spooked me all night!

The next morning brought us to Chebisa, the prettiest highland village I have seen. Against the backdrop of the snow-covered peaks of Jichu Drake (6850 metres) and Tshering Gang (6532 metres) and a brilliant blue sky, the village houses nestle beside a stream, amidst barley fields and grassy meadows. I had lunch with the villagers, and thought I could happily live in Chebisa the rest of my life—but not in winter! The villagers proudly recalled the visit of the king and queen of Sweden, who had stayed here some years earlier.

From Chebisa we walked on to another village called Gangyul, the rocks around which boast extraordinary natural formations— one in the shape of a perfect pair of bull's horns, and the other like the head of a bull. These, I was told, were miraculously created by Tsangpa Gyare, who in 1189 founded the Drukpa Kargyupa sect of Buddhism, the official religion of the Bhutanese state. The locals believe that Tsangpa Gyare arrived here riding a bull, and left these rocks as souvenirs of his visit. From Gangyul, a strenuous climb over the Gombula Pass (4440 metres) brought us on the route to Lingzhi. At the outskirts of Lingzhi we witnessed another yak fight—between a black animal and a white one. This time, I took good care to stay well out of their way. The white yak lost, and perhaps it was an ill omen of sorts, for on reaching Lingzhi our best pack mule, Tshering Jum, dropped dead.

Lingzhi Dzong is perched on a high spur, with rolling hills on all sides, and the great peaks of Mount Tshering Gang and Mount Jichu Drake clearly visible to its north. Originally constructed in 1222, it was rebuilt by Zhabdrung Ngawang Namgyel in 1647, to defend this frontier against invasions from the north. It is still a working dzong, housing the offices of the *dungpa* (administrator) of Lingzhi gewog (county), as well as its small monk body. The dungpa rides up to the dzong from his home at the base of the hill every day—probably one of the few bureaucrats in the world who commutes to work on horseback. The monks joined us in prayers for the soul of our poor dead mule Tshering Jum, and then we went to meet the eighty-nine children and three teachers at the Lingzhi school. The children, most of whose parents are yak herders and so lead peripatetic lives, board at the school. I was not surprised to learn that this boarding school, which fills a real need in the lives of the yak-herding community, had been set up by Prince Namgyel Wangchuck, the uncle of the King, who has travelled on foot all over the country to look after the welfare of the people.

Moving on from Lingzhi, I began the toughest climb of my trip so far, over the Ngelela Pass at 5100 metres. It was windy and bitterly cold at the top. We were met there by the gup of Soe, a settlement a day's walk downhill, who told us that a snow leopard had been spotted on the pass just a few days earlier. The gup's late grandfather, Soep Jou, was a familiar figure to our family. He was the legendary strongman of the area, able to pick up a sack of rice with his teeth and load it on to the horse. When the King had first come to this region, Soep Jou had given him his white yak to ride, and the King had looked after Soep Jou's welfare until his death two years earlier.

Descending from the Ngelela Pass, I made a quick detour to the Tsophu lake, which looked like a sapphire ringed by enormous diamonds. On this cloudless autumn day, my heart soared as I saw the mountains Jichu Drake, Chomolhari and Tshering Gang reflected in Tsophu's shimmering blue waters. Within an hour I reached my campsite at Jangothang, at the foot of Mt Chomolhari. The ruins of an old dzong still stand above the campsite—it was where the caravans of Bhutanese mule traders would stop on their way back from Tibet to pay tax in the form of a certain amount of salt to the dungpa of the dzong. Phari in Tibet is just a day's walk from here. Fields of medicinal herbs are tended and harvested in the region around Jangothang, and much of their produce supplied to the National Institute of Traditional Medicine in Thimphu. The yak herders I met here have taken enthusiastically to growing these herbs, which provide a welcome new source of income.

The last stretch of my tour, from Jangothang to the road-head at Paro, is a well-travelled route, a favourite with foreign visitors looking for a short trek that would give them a glimpse of snow peaks, alpine lakes, and meadows filled with herds of yaks. The roar of the rushing river, the gold of the birch trees in their autumn colours, the fragrance of pine, and the songs of the yak herders floating over the mountains created a symphony of colour, scent and sound that filled my senses all the way to Paro—a perfect finale to the memorable days I had spent among the yak herders of Laya and Lingzhi, whose lives have a unique and beautiful rhythm and harmony.

CHAPTER 12

HEAVENLY LAKES

Perhaps the most difficult place to get to in Bhutan is Lunana, in our far northern highlands. But for those who brave the journey, the rewards are fabulous. Lunana is a land of peaks and glaciers, studded with dozens of jewel-like lakes, in every shade of turquoise, jade, aquamarine and emerald. Watching over this landscape, almost unearthly in its primeval grandeur, is Mt Gangkar Puensum (7541 metres), our sacred mountain. The highest peak in Bhutan, it has never been scaled, and in fact remains the highest unclimbed peak in the world. We pray that this abode of the gods remains forever unsullied by the footprints of human beings.

As awesome as the land are its people—the Lunaps are a handsome people, known for their physical stamina, independent spirit and difficult temperament. Spurning the comfort and ease of life in the more temperate valleys, they have a strong attachment to their land, and take pride in their ability to making a living in its harsh environment. Like the people of Laya and Lingzhi, most Lunaps too are yak herders.

In 1994, Lunana literally burst into our consciousness when unusually warm spring weather resulted in a sudden meltdown of the glaciers which flow into one of Lunana's lakes, Lugge Tsho. This caused the lake to burst its boundaries with tremendous force, causing a flash flood of the Phochhu river far downstream in Punakha. Twenty-three people working on the restoration of Punakha Dzong were drowned in the flood. The lake-burst also caused a devastating change in the ecology of Lunana, turning rich pastureland into high-altitude sandy desert. Since then, a major project has been undertaken to study the ice-melting patterns and prevent similar flash floods in the future, by creating drainage systems for the lakes.

Getting to Lunana involves at least eight days of walking, over some extremely treacherous trails and dauntingly steep passes. In fact, seasoned international trekkers regard the 'Snowman's Trek' to Lunana as one of the most difficult in the world. My own dream of going to Lunana seemed more unattainable with each passing year. In early 2002, my face had swelled up like a cabbage during a visit to the mountains of Soe, near the base of Mt Chomolhari. I realized that I could no longer count on being impervious to the effects of high altitude, nor could I put off my plans to go to Lunana—I was forty-seven years old; it was now or never. And so, in the summer of that year, I set off for this faraway land, 'somewhere, over the rainbow . . .'

My journey to Lunana began with a pilgrimage to a hallowed site— the cave temple at Geon Tsephu, a day's ride from the Punakha Valley. (I was riding, and not walking, because this terrain is infested by leeches, of which I have a horror.) The temple site is said to have been blessed by Guru Padmasambhava when he came here in the eighth century, and dedicated to his consort Yeshe Tshogyel. Legend has it that the Guru discovered a 'spring of immortality' here, and 100,000 dakinis congregated here during his visit. Zhabdrung Ngawang Namgyel had visited this cave in the seventeenth century and wished to build a temple here, but his wish was only realized after his death, by Desi Tenzin Rabgye. The old temple was

restored in the 1950s by Queen Phuntsho Choden, the wife of
Bhutan's second king, who spent two months here in meditation.
My own visit to the temple was a hurried one for I had spotted
leeches right beside the altar; so after seeking the Guru's blessings
for our journey, we continued on to Ramina, the first hamlet in
Lunana gewog (county), where we camped for the night. It poured
with rain that night, and as I sat in my dripping tent I feared our
expedition to the Lunana highlands would be aborted.

Luckily, the sun shone brightly the next morning and we made
an early start, for we had a long day's march to our campsite at
Jaziphu. Accompanying us were porters from Lunana and Goen
Shari, a village on the way to Gasa. Leading the porters was the tall
and handsome young Phurba, reputed to be the strongest man in
Lunana—he could effortlessly carry a horse's load on his back, and
still be several strides ahead of the rest of us. As soon as we crossed
the stream that demarcated leech territory from the no-leech zone I
began to feel much more energetic. Our trail led us gradually uphill
to a small pass, and to our west I saw the first of many lakes. Then
began the climb over a stretch locally known as the 'Iron Ladder',
which was almost vertical and very slippery, with water trickling
down the stones—it required utmost caution and total concentration
to negotiate.

Thankfully, we traversed the Iron Ladder without mishap, and
our campsite at Jaziphu Valley soon came in sight, with many rock
caves around it and mist-covered mountains to its left. The Lunana
porters, on familiar ground, quickly 'booked' the caves where they
would spend the night, while the porters from Goen looked lost and
tired—they had climbed the Iron Ladder with great trepidation,
leaving their loads at the bottom. Though darkness had fallen, our
Lunana porters came to the rescue; they went back down the Iron
Ladder and returned safely with all our luggage. I slept soundly in
my sleeping bag in the lee of a huge rock, after a dinner of rice with
ema datsi (chillies and cheese)—the ultimate comfort food for us
Bhutanese!

The next morning, the second day of our journey, we caught our
first glimpse of the magical Lunana landscape. Just two hours' walk
from our campsite at Jaziphu, we came upon Yue Tsho (Turquoise

Lake). Shaped like a perfect conch shell, it was fed by water from a lake higher up, Ser Tsho, or Golden Lake. The Yue Tsho lake was deep and dark greeny-blue, surrounded by rocks. After this, our trail deteriorated sharply—a long stretch of mud and slush, through which we struggled.

We felt less sorry for ourselves when we spotted in the distance the desolate, forbidding track to Yusena, the most isolated settlement in Bhutan. It would have taken two and a half days' walk to get there, over two high passes. The track to Yusena is too narrow for fully grown cattle to walk on, so only small calves are taken up. Even rice and other food grains are carried there a little at a time, hidden in crevices in the cliff to be gradually retrieved later. There are now only three households left in Yusena, with a total of twelve people, when a few years earlier there were fifteen households. Only one government official—an intrepid community health technician, carrying essential medical supplies and vaccines—has actually managed to make it all the way to Yusena. The top district official accompanied by seven able-bodied men had given up after a week-long attempt and turned back. I found myself wondering about the lives of the twelve people left in Yusena, who continue to cling to a way of life that is becoming increasingly untenable. They must be very self-sufficient indeed, very attached to their land—and from time to time they must definitely be getting badly on each other's nerves!

As we neared our campsite at Jangsa, the trail became easier and the landscape enchanting, with moss-covered rocks around a sparkling stream, the ground studded with a carpet of flowers—primulas, fritillaries, yellow poppies, tiny asters and many other varieties of exquisite alpine plants. Our campsite was at the foot of the Gangzhula Pass and a difficult climb lay ahead the next day. But that evening, we relaxed as we visited the herders and their families in their black wool tents, admired their handsome yaks and watched the women churning butter in cylindrical wooden churns and making cheese by pressing the whey between large, round stones. The butter and cheese would be bartered for food grains, tea and other essentials that the herders need.

Early the next morning, as we began our ascent of the Gangzhula

Pass, we climbed past three small turquoise lakes close to each other, at a place called 'Sum To Shisa' (where three died), so called because a family of three had perished there in a sudden snowstorm. I was shown another spot where a woman had died and a cave above the track where a man had died a few years earlier—both from exposure to the cold. We saw two more lakes before we reached the top of the Gangzhula Pass (5000 metres) which was deep in snow. We strung prayer flags for the King on the highest point at the pass, and then slowly and silently focused on our footsteps as we negotiated the icy terrain. I was told that twelve young men and fifteen yaks had fallen into crevices and died here not long ago. The Lunap custom is that if a companion dies in the snow, the one who reaches home safely would deny that the other had been with him.

Wet and shivering with cold, I began to feel lightheaded and nauseous, but took two Tylenols and carried on until the Gangzhula Pass was behind us. Lunch was cold rice and radish, which we shared with the exhausted porters. All our packhorses had been sent back before we crossed the Gangzhula. The descent from the pass was very steep and seemed never-ending, and it was a great relief to arrive at our camp in a pretty forested area, with the Woche hot springs nearby. It had been a long and exhausting day, but I had seen five beautiful lakes. I was too tired to go to the springs for a soak, and had the hot water brought to my tent. My face had swelled up, and I took Diamox to counter the effects of the altitude.

The next morning I had a delightful surprise—my old friend Galey, the chocolate-coloured yak from Laya, was waiting for me with his owner Tenzin. A Lunana yak herder, seventy-year-old Ap Tshering, also arrived with his two yaks for us to ride. I rode Galey to meet the people of Woche village, for whom I had brought fleece blankets—one blanket for each of the ten households in the village. From Woche, the porters from Goen Shari returned home, taking with them a renewed appreciation of the relative ease of their lives in the more temperate valleys lower down, and a grudging respect for the grit and stamina of the Lunaps.

Leaving Woche, we crossed a small pass, the Kechila at 4666 metres, and a tiny lake, before beginning the descent to Threga. As I walked down I turned on my radio, for I had requested the Bhutan

Broadcasting Service (BBS) to play my three favourite songs for my elder brother Sangay, who at that time was traversing Bhutan on foot from east to west, walking from Tashigang in eastern Bhutan to Thimphu, with thirty-seven kilos on his back. Sangay, as minister for health and education, was walking to raise funds for the Health Trust Fund that had been established by our King. (His walk catalysed an effort that has so far resulted in 18 million dollars for the fund.) The BBS reaches the most remote parts of the country, and is much used by families and friends who are scattered at great distances from each other, to keep in touch.

We passed another lake and a little further down we came to a sacred rock called Do Mo Tabsa, with a chorten near it—there is a narrow crevice in the rock into which one is supposed to throw a coin for good luck, and if the coin misses the crevice it is not a good omen. I said a silent prayer, took careful aim—and made it! Past the chorten, I met yak herders from the tiny hamlets of Threga and Shanza, and gave them the fleece blankets I had brought for them. Barley and a few root vegetables are all that can grow on their land, they told me, adding that the floods in 1994 had destroyed their pasturelands, forcing them to climb higher and higher in search of food for their animals.

Soon after we left Shanza, passing a beautiful little watermill, the devastation wrought by the floods became evident—what used to be fertile pastureland until 1994 was now a wide sandy riverbed. Riding across it in the twilight on Galey's broad and comfortable back, I thought it would have been more fitting to ride a camel on such terrain. We camped that night, our fifth night on this tour, near the community school at Lheydi—the centre of Lunana gewog, with nine households. Our host Geon Tsering, the chimi (member of Bhutan's National Assembly) of Lunana, was a handsome man with two front teeth missing. I soon learned how he lost his teeth. He had been a monk at Gasa Dzong until, at the age of twenty-seven, he had married his sixteen-year-old neighbour, the sister of the young strongman Phurba, our travelling companion from the very first day of this journey. After his marriage, Geon Tsering had taken to the pleasures of the lay life—especially wine and women—with gusto. His distraught young wife complained to her brother, whose powerful punch knocked out Geon Tsering's teeth. I was told that he had never strayed since that day!

The next morning, I came across an Austrian team that had arrived by helicopter two days earlier to study the rate of glacial melt and the drainage system of the lakes. They told me that it would take at least fifteen years for the sandy wasteland to become pastureland again. Meanwhile, the yaks were going hungry. People from the twenty-two households in neighbouring villages had also gathered at Lheydi, and they expressed their distress that their yaks were now forced to graze even on steep cliffsides, which caused many of them to fall to their deaths. They also pressed for a new mule track to be built following the course of the Phochhu river, which would then considerably shorten their journey, bringing them within 'an arrow's distance' from Punakha. I had already seen enough of life in Lunana to realize how even the rough mule track they wanted would vastly improve the food security and medical facilities of the people.

After a happy morning with the twenty-two students and two teachers at the Lheydi community school, sharing the apples I had brought, it was time to move on again, following the course of the river, and walking uphill to Tshodzong, three hours away. A woman and two children living in the last house in Tshodzong village were drowned in the 1994 flash flood. The village, consisting of twenty-six houses, all made of stone, surrounds the old dzong which is said to date to the early seventeenth century. There is a temple in the dzong's three-storeyed central tower, filled with beautiful images and exquisite old thangkas, including a rare one of Zhabdrung Ngawang Namgyel as a young man (he is usually depicted with a long grey beard). As always, when visiting temples in the most remote corners of the country, I was struck by the treasures they contain, of great antiquity and artistic quality, treasures that the world's great museums would love to display, but which remain unknown to the outside world. I hope the day never comes when these objects, imbued with the aura of centuries of faith and devotion, will have to be locked away for safety from art thieves. Tshodzong looked like a lost Eden, framed against a cerulean sky and the snow peaks of Table Mountain (7000 metres).

A little past Tshodzong we crossed an enormous sandy stretch covering four kilometres—again a result of the 1994 floods—and walked on towards Thanza where we were to spend the night. At 4100 metres, Thanza is the highest and northernmost village in Bhutan, and it was dark when we reached—it had been over ten hours since we had left Lheydi that morning. The next morning, the seventh day of our tour, I woke up very early, feeling all of my forty-seven years. I felt I could do nothing that day—I was tired from walking, and even from meeting and talking to so many different sets of villagers. But as I emerged from my tent, my mood lifted—before my eyes was the sublime sight of the rising sun touching the peaks of Mt Thanzala. Fortified by a hurried breakfast of rice and ema datsi, I rode yak Galey up the hill in front of our camp, beyond which there were three lakes. Accompanying us was our other yak-herder friend, the seventy-year-old Ap Tshering. This morning, he was desolate because he had lost his favourite black leather jacket somewhere near Lheydi the previous day. Despite his years, Ap Tshering was a dashing fellow who took great pride in his appearance—I called him Hrithik Roshan because, like the Bollywood film star, he had six fingers on one hand. He cheered up when I gave him a smart new fleece jacket.

As we rode uphill, the song of a yak herder floated in the clear, still air. There is something haunting about the yak herders' songs, whether in Laya or Lunana, and the song I heard this morning was so moving and poetic that I wrote down the words. It's the lament of a male yak as he awaits slaughter. Here is an English translation:

Yak Lhadar's Lament

How beautiful is Yak Legpai Lhadar's face
Yak Legpai Lhadar, the god-sent calf
Shall I describe my home and my paths?

If I should tell you of my home and my paths
They are up high, on the snow-capped mountains
And the highland meadow of the *sershog* flower
Where blossoms bloom, oh there's my home

I roam and graze on alpine grass
And drink the waters of glacial lakes
And when I dance and prance in joy
I dance at the foot of distant mountains

Then came the command of a powerful lord
A lord with a sword that dangled from his waist
He came to take Yak Legpai Lhadar
Lhadar has no choice, no choice but to go

When came the time and the turn for slaughter
The turn fell on me, Yak Legpai Lhadar
The snow-covered peaks above, how high!
And Lhadar's tree of life, how low!

(Translated into English by Dorji Penjore)

After a while, I got down from my yak and began walking along the riverbed which was filled with jagged and loose stones after the flood—it was a veritable obstacle course, and my feet were in agony. After nearly four hours of walking, I arrived at Lugge Tsho lake—this was the lake that had burst its banks and caused such devastation in 1994. The scenery was spectacular, with towering snow-capped peaks to the north of the turquoise lake, and in their presence I felt small and insignificant, like the tiny heart-shaped stone I had found on the banks of the lake, and now put in my pocket as a talisman. I put some water from the lake on my head, prostrated five times in obeisance to the deity of the lake and put eight coins in the water as an offering. I had lunch beside the lake, in the company of an adventurous sixty-one-year-old Japanese professor and his two students, who were also studying methods of gently draining the overflow from the lakes. Great blocks of melting ice kept falling into the lake with resounding *thunk-clunk* sounds.

We walked on to see two more lakes that morning—the deep-blue Thothormey Tsho, the largest of Lunana's glacial lakes, with huge black stones piled up on its sides; and the jade-green Rapsthrang Tsho below it, surrounded by juniper trees and ringed by snow-capped peaks. I was to learn a couple of years later that both these lakes bore the seeds of future disaster. With global warming, the Thothormey glacier and its surrounding snowfields are melting, the water level in Thothormey Tsho and Rapsthrang Tsho is rising dangerously high, and if the two lakes were to burst their banks they would unleash 53 million cubic metres of water, causing a flood with three times the ferocity of the one in 1994. There are elaborate—and expensive—plans to manually lower the water level of Thothormey Tsho, and I hope they are completed before disaster strikes again.

But that morning, the waters of both lakes were limpid and tranquil, with the mountains reflected in them. Thinley, a forest guard of the Jigme Dorji National Park, who was keeping a close watch on the lakes and glaciers, asked me if I would name the peak to the right of the Gongtola Range, popularly known as the Table Mountain, which was clearly visible from where we stood. I promptly and happily named it Gangchen Singye—Great Mountain Singye—after our King, who is like a mighty mountain for his people, always there to shoulder their burdens.

Back at our campsite in Thanza that evening, we had a get-together round the campfire with families from all the villages in the neighbourhood, and listened to the stories of seventy-four-year-old Ap Chethey, who told us how he and others from his village used to cross over the border into Tibet to trade their goods, by cutting steps into the ice-covered mountain slopes, roping themselves together. The border with Tibet has, of course, been closed since 1959. Handing over 101 fleece blankets, and sets of kiras and ghos for the elderly people of the area, we finally managed to lighten our luggage loads considerably.

The next day our destination was Tshorim lake, a mostly uphill walk, but I didn't make it—I fell violently ill with stomach cramps and we had to stop and set up an 'emergency' camp en route. The next morning I felt better and willed myself to continue—'Mind over matter,' I kept repeating to myself. I slowly got my energy back as we reached Tshorim, a long, sparkling blue lake framed by a panoramic view of the Gongphula Range. We then crossed the Gongphula Pass at 5345 metres and descended near the base camp of our sacred Mt Gangkar Puensum. Our campsite was covered with flowering *selu* (dwarf rhododendron bushes)—no trees grow at this altitude, for we were still above the treeline, and the night was bitterly cold.

The next morning dawned bright and clear, and it was a delight to walk along the wide valley scattered with flowers. A two-hour trek brought us right to the base of Gangkar Puensum, the source of three rivers that have brought life and prosperity to Bhutan—the Chamkarchhu of Bumthang, the Kurichhu of Mongar and the Mangdechhu of Tongsa. The waters of these rivers provide the hydroelectric power that is Bhutan's main source of wealth. As I stood before the great mountain, I hoped my children would come here one day to experience the unique beauty of this corner of their country. As for myself, I realized sadly that I would not come this way again—the effects of the altitude had begun to take their toll. I took Diamox to reduce the oedema, the side-effects of which were a strange tingling sensation on my tongue, hands and feet. That day we encountered many caravans of yak herders on their way to the higher pasturelands of Lunana. Among them was a young mother with her baby girl strapped to her back. The little one had the same birthday as me. She had not yet been named, and her mother asked me to choose a name. I gave her my own name, Dorji Wangmo— a way of fulfilling my wish to leave behind a little bit of myself in Lunana. We spent that night, our tenth on this journey, at a yak herders' encampment at Menchugang at 4210 metres.

The following day we faced a very challenging climb over the Rimola Pass, and I slowly inched my way up, using a walking stick for support. When I finally reached the top, I placed a large stone on top of the mound that other travellers had left and, as is the custom when one crosses a particularly dangerous or tiring stretch of a journey, all of us exclaimed '*Lha Gelo!*'—the Gods are victorious—in exhilaration. We walked on for a few hours through a stretch of red earth and sand before beginning our next ascent, over the Sakala Pass at 4820 metres. The sight of a lovely jade-green lake shaped like a tree revived our sagging spirits and aching muscles as we toiled up the pass, as did a large stone shaped just like a fat shark with its jaws open. It began to snow and a thick mist descended as we came down to our camp at Waruthang (4550 metres) and holed up to rest for the night.

A half-hour climb the next morning led us to the Juela Pass, after which we descended through dense rhododendron and juniper forest, where a rare treat awaited us—the sight of five monal pheasants perched on a tree. We stopped in our tracks, and filled our eyes with the sight of these most beautiful of Himalayan birds, with their iridescent blue, gold, red and yellow feathers, and the distinctive crest on their heads. The feathers of the monal are greatly prized by archers, as they are used to make the best fletches for arrows. A short while later we descended to the hot springs at Dur at 3310 metres. It was blissful to sink into the warm pool and soak one's aches and pains away. We enjoyed the therapeutic benefits and picturesque surroundings of Dur for three days, bracing ourselves for the daunting last leg of our journey, which would bring us down into the wide and gentle valleys of Bumthang in central Bhutan.

We certainly needed all our reserves of strength the next morning as we struggled up the Gorthungla Pass at 4470 metres. It was snowing heavily, the trail was steep, slippery and slushy, and as we laboured through the mist and snow, we felt as though we were in a scene from that old movie classic, *Lost Horizon*. On the way, we found welcome shelter in a yak herdsman's hut, huddled round his yak dung fire to have our lunch, and then continued on our way, following the course of the Chamkarchhu river.

Soon we came upon a group of men who were on a pasture development survey, and one of them, a young man, was bloated and delirious with severe altitude sickness. They were rushing him down to a lower altitude. It was fortunate that we had a doctor in our group and an oxygen cylinder and, if our paths had not crossed at this moment, he would probably have lost his life. To see him rally round enough to survive the journey up to the road-head, where our cars waited, was a wonderful finale to our Lunana odyssey. We accompanied him to the hospital at Bumthang, and within a short while he was able to speak. I asked him if he remembered what he had experienced when he was so close to death. His response was not quite the poetic or philosophical one I had expected: 'Yes,' he said, 'I was imagining how my girlfriend would react when she heard that I had died!'

Throughout our trek, crossing several high passes and walking on dangerous trails from which so many had fallen to their deaths, I could only give fervent thanks that no one in my party had suffered severe altitude sickness or any other serious ailment when the nearest medical facilities were several days' walk away. Altitude sickness is unpredictable and can even strike the young and fit who have never suffered it in the past. I cannot emphasize how important it is to descend quickly to lower altitudes if one is suffering from severe symptoms of oedema and disorientation—our young friend whom we rescued had waited until it was almost too late.

I followed a few simple rules that I think helped me keep well enough to complete this journey. I kept well-hydrated with water and ate very sparingly, for nothing saps one's energy more surely than a heavy meal. I walked at a slow and steady pace, and was not ashamed to stop for short breaks when I was really tired—it is when one is tired or in a hurry that one tends to miss one's step and have accidents. And I believe mental discipline on such a journey is as important as physical discipline—one's stamina depends a great deal on one's state of mind. My journey to Lunana had taught me, among many other things, that we are all capable of much more than we think we are.

CHAPTER 13

THE VALLEYS OF
THE BROKPAS

Once upon a time, in the Tshona region of southern Tibet, there lived a tyrannical chieftain called Yarsang. One day, he thought up a diabolical new way to oppress his people—he ordered them to cut down the mountain in front of his palace, so that more sunlight would come into his rooms. The people toiled for years at this back-breaking task, from sunrise to sunset, but were barely able to make a dent in the mountain. In desperation, they gathered together one evening to discuss what they should do. Among those present was a beautiful young woman, Aum Jomo, who spoke up: 'Wouldn't it be easier to cut off the soft head of the chieftain, than to cut down the hard, rocky mountain?' she said. Her logic was irrefutable.

And so the people of Tshona arranged a grand feast in honour of the chieftain, with plenty to eat and drink. As a grand finale, they announced that they would perform the spectacular sword dance for which the young men of the region were renowned. As the chieftain watched in a drunken stupor, they took out their swords and after a few twirls and flourishes advanced on him and cut off his head. After the deed was done, the people realized that they had to flee

Tshona, and Aum Jomo, together with their revered Lama Jarepa, offered to lead them to a new home.

Travelling for several months through snowbound mountains and dense forests, crossing roaring rivers and deep gorges, and taking their yaks and sheep with them, the refugees finally arrived at the base of a very high pass. The strongest and fittest people and animals managed to climb over the pass, where they found a beautiful uninhabited plateau covered with shrubs. They set the shrubs on fire to clear the land, and settled down there. The place was named Merak, which means 'set on fire'. But the majority were too tired to even attempt to cross the pass and decided to turn back. (The pass, which they named the Nyakchungla, means 'tired'.) On their way back they climbed a small hill and came upon a wide and beautiful flat valley covered with bamboo and surrounded by rhododendrons, and realized that they had at last found their promised land. They named it Sakteng which means 'the land on the top'.

And thus were established the two remote settlements of Merak and Sakteng in the extreme east of Bhutan, whose people, the Brokpas, have retained their unique traditions and customs. Like the people of Laya, Lingzhi and Lunana, they too are primarily yak herders. Aum Jomo, who led them out of slavery in Tibet into these undiscovered valleys in Bhutan, is now worshipped by the Brokpas as their deity. Ancient texts preserved in their monasteries, as well as oral traditions, corroborate this account of the origin of the Brokpas of Merak and Sakteng, though there is some debate about the date of their arrival—some sources say they came in the seventh century, others say the fifteenth or sixteenth century. My visit to Merak and Sakteng in May 2001 turned out to be a 'magical mystery tour' (to use the words of the old Beatles' song), full of memorable and marvellous new experiences.

Merak and Sakteng are in Tashigang district. The bustling town of Tashigang, the district headquarters, is dominated by its dzong, built in 1656, and dramatically situated on a high spur overlooking the deep gorge of the Dangmechhu river. The Brokpas of Merak and Sakteng are a familiar sight in Tashigang town in winter, where they come down to trade their yak products for rice and other goods.

They can be seen strolling around town with an air of great confidence, happily high on ara, their good humour and infectious laughter always attracting a crowd around them. The Brokpas are impossible to miss, because they dress like no one else in Bhutan. Most distinctive of all is their headgear known as the *tsipee cham*— a round, black felt hat, rather like a French beret, with five long tail-like projections from the rim. These serve as gutters that are supposed to drain away the rainwater from their faces. The Brokpa men wear belted red wool jackets, felt shorts, leather leggings and knee-high wool and leather boots. Over this, they wear a tunic of deerskin or calf hide. This costume protects them from thorny bushes and scrub when they go into the forests to round up their yaks. A small, round piece of felt hangs from the belt, to be used as a handy waterproof cushion. The Brokpa women wear a pink and white striped raw-silk dress, a long-sleeved red shirt with lovely flower and animal motifs woven on it and, in cold weather, a black wool jacket. A black wool apron is tied on their back, to serve as a portable mat and for extra warmth. Both men and women have large turquoise stones dangling from their ears—they believe the turquoise ensures that after death they will never be short of water, to quench the soul's thirst.

My journey on foot from Tashigang to Sakteng and Merak began with a most curious incident for which there is no rational explanation. On the second day of my trek I went to visit the beautiful old temple of Lhamoi Gompa near the village of Threlphu, where I had spent the night. It held one of the most sublime Buddha images I have ever seen. The wooden floor in front of its altar was indented with the foot imprints of a devotee who had prostrated before it thousands of times. Exquisite murals covered the walls, and the temple's Zhabdrung image too was unique, its expression a superb mixture of amusement and sternness. But when I came out of the temple, I suddenly felt very unwell. I was overcome with nausea, and sat down by myself in a field of corn, to pull myself together before meeting the villagers who were waiting for me at the end of the field.

I saw a brown bull and a black one with their horns locked in fierce combat in the centre of the field. Soon the brown bull got the upper hand, and chased the black one right down to the end of the terraced fields. After a while, I was able to haul myself up for a brief meeting with the villagers, and then as I walked on my companions noticed blood trickling down my right temple. I wiped off the blood and was mystified as to its source, for there was no cut, scratch or insect bite to account for it. As soon as we reached camp at Kangpara, I collapsed in bed, feeling too ill to sit up, speak or eat.

Fortunately, I felt better the next morning and was able to keep my engagement at Sherubtse College in Kanglung, the premier institute for higher education in Bhutan. At the college, I recounted my bizarre experience to the head abbot of Tashigang and a learned local lama. Both of them immediately had an explanation for the mysterious bleeding from my temple—they said the Za (the planetary deity) of Lhamoi Gompa had taken a fancy to me, as a result of which I could have ended up paralysed or dead. But, according to their interpretation, the victory of the brown bull over the black one soon after I came out of Lhamoi Gompa was an omen that I was being protected by the deity of Talo, who had succeeded in driving out the Za. The belief in the force of supernatural powers and spirits is particularly strong in eastern Bhutan, and their explanation of my sudden and mysterious affliction was offered with absolute conviction. I still don't know what to make of this intriguing experience, but I will think twice before going to Lhamoi Gompa again!

The next morning I was back on the road again, stopping at a shop to buy five needles, which I carefully put into my purse—needles are regarded as symbols of life, and they were my talismans for this trip. A jolly group of Brokpas was waiting along the road with casks full of ara brewed from barley, with which they plied us insistently. I couldn't refuse this traditional offer of hospitality and friendship, so I resorted to the subterfuge of taking a small sip and stealthily letting the rest of the brew trickle through my fingers on to the hem of my kira. For the rest of the day I stank like an alcoholic, but was delighted to discover that the ara also proved most effective in keeping leeches away—and this was a trail absolutely crawling with the horrid creatures. My usual leech-deterrent recipe is a mixture of Dettol, salt and tobacco sprayed on my socks and the hem of my kira.

Our route for the first few hours took us through farms in the lowlands before the climb to Sakteng began. The farmers complained bitterly about the destruction of their crops by the growing population of wild boar and bears, a perennial dilemma in Bhutan where our religion forbids the killing of any living being. Soon our trail led uphill, much of it through forests of rhododendron which, at this time of the year, were in spectacular bloom. It was pouring with rain by the time we reached our camp at Jongthang. But the sun shone the next morning, and the forest sparkled with raindrops, as though the trees were dripping diamonds. The rhododendron blooms— scarlet, pink, yellow, mauve, white and pale orange—had an unearthly beauty glimpsed through patches of mist. Not for nothing was Sakteng's other name Beyul Tama Jang—the Hidden Paradise of the Rhododendron Blossom.

After a hard climb, which brought us to an altitude of 3000 metres, the sight of a long stone *mani* wall signalled that we had almost reached our destination. A short while later Sakteng suddenly came into view—a gentle valley bathed in a golden light, with its stone houses huddled close together and its temples on the ridge above. A Dakota plane had crashed near the valley in the 1960s, and every last bit of metal from the wreckage had been salvaged, to be ingeniously fashioned into doorframes, cooking utensils, stoves and ladders by the people of Sakteng. The silvery glint of the metal, the grey shingle roofs, the green meadows dotted with black yaks and the ubiquitous red jackets of the Brokpas created an enchanting palette of colours.

My camp was in the centre of a wide green meadow, with a

fence around it for privacy, woven of leafy branches. A wood-burning stove made my enclosure delightfully warm, and I slept soundly. The next morning we climbed up the hill to two historic Sakteng temples, our path strewn with wild strawberries and tiny purple flowers. Eleven young girls from Sakteng accompanied us, serenading us all the way. Borangtse Temple is the oldest in the region, believed to have been established by Lama Jarepa who, along with Aum Jomo, had guided the people of Tshona to Sakteng and Merak. The original temple, which was seven-storeyed, had caught fire and burned, but the ancient sacred texts had been saved, as had the precious statues of Guru Padmasambhava and of Zambala, the God of Wealth. They have pride of place on Borangtse's altar. More imposing is the second temple, Kusho Guru Lhakhang, whose treasures include superb paintings of local deities, including Aum Jomo. She wears silken robes, jewels and a beatific expression, and rides a swift-footed mule. In her right hand she holds a banner, while her left hand holds a skull-bowl filled with gems. In her wrathful form, when she subdues demons, Aum Jomo is depicted as blue-black, with three glaring eyes, and is poised on crocodile and snake skins. I enjoyed the panoramic view of Sakteng from this temple, before heading to the upper corner of the valley to watch cheese being made in a yak herder's wooden cabin.

We spent a delightful couple of hours with the herders as they churned butter, singing a song to keep the rhythm of the churning. We also watched them prepare their famous fermented cheese, *zethoey*. The fresh cheese is sewn into yak-hide bags and kept in a warm place to mature—the older the cheese, the stronger the taste. Zethoey is a much-prized delicacy in Bhutan, though an acquired taste for the uninitiated, like the blue or brie cheeses of Europe. As we tasted their cheese, the yak herders and their wives subjected us to a typical Sakteng custom—taking us completely by surprise, they rubbed flour on our face and hair. This is the Brokpa way of wishing long life, since the white flour symbolizes the white hair of old age. We presented a ridiculous sight—and much comic relief to the people of Sakteng—as we headed back to our camp in the rain, the flour streaking down our faces.

Back in the village, we visited several houses, including that of the venerable religious head of the village, the Sakteng Trulku. In one house we watched the long and meticulous process by which their trademark tsipee cham caps are made. About 300 grams of yak hair is first untangled and cleaned, and then packed into a small, round pot with a liquid that serves as a binder—either whey or the residue from making grain alcohol. It is amazing how effectively this binds the hair into a mat. The mixture is then pounded and kneaded until it forms a compressed round wafer. Five points at the rim are pulled out to make tails and another bunch of yak hair is added to these and rolled to the required length, making the cap look like a giant black spider. Once the cap is dry, the tsipee cham is ready.

The highlight of the cultural show put on by the Brokpas for us was the Yak Cham, a spectacular dance that is more like a pantomime. It was performed by five masked men who danced vigorously to the beat of drums. Then two other dancers appeared, covered with a black blanket and sporting the horned head of a yak. Carrying an image of Aum Jomo on their back, they sang lyrical hymns in praise of their pastoral life, their deities, and their beloved yaks, and enacted the story of their flight from Tibet, led by Aum Jomo. These dances were interspersed with hilarious interludes demonstrating the perils of loading a yak. In real life too this is often an amusing sight, as the herder struggles with this great beast, who tries every tactic he knows to throw off his load, including rolling on the ground to smash the contents of the saddlebags. The Brokpas are brilliant mimics with a great sense of the comic, and we laughed until our sides ached as we watched their antics.

The warm and easy hospitality of the people of Sakteng had made us feel so much at home that it was hard to leave after just two days. As we set off for Merak the next morning, the women of Sakteng sang a farewell song and, as is their custom, waved their scarves at us until we were out of sight.

The walk from Sakteng to Merak was a real test of fitness and endurance, over the dreaded and aptly named Nyakchungla Pass, from where Aum Jomo's tired refugees had turned back. We had to keep stopping to take deep breaths, counting to 150, and then to 300 as we neared the top of the pass, at 4140 metres. Merak, at an altitude of 3517 metres, is a smaller and narrower valley than Sakteng, and the people looked taller and stronger—not surprisingly, as they are the descendants of the fittest group among the refugees who came here with Aum Jomo. I was fascinated by the species of juniper that grew around Merak, shaped like little pyramids—or like the hat that high lamas wear, as the Brokpas of Merak say. The houses in Merak are in the centre of the valley, facing a river. That night, as I slept in my tent, I had a wonderful dream, of a gracious lady who gave me her necklace of corals and zees and a gold bracelet from her wrist. I like to think it was Aum Jomo, welcoming us to her abode.

Merak's main temple, the Samtenling Lhakhang, built in 1890, is full of murals and contains a rare treasure—eighteen volumes of handwritten scriptures, which were brought from Tibet by Aum Jomo. A fabulous temple near Merak is Gengo Lhakhang, which dates to 1650, with many holy relics, including a row of exquisite copper and wooden chortens. It was built by a famous Merak lama, Lodey Gyatso, who also built the great monastery of Tawang just across the border in India's Arunachal Pradesh province.

In Merak, as in Laya, the custom of polyandry is not uncommon. I visited the house of a forty-nine-year-old woman who is married to three brothers, the youngest one just a few years older than her eldest daughter. They are a prosperous family and, judging from the easy camaraderie that prevailed among the three husbands and all the children, a happy one. The mother of the three husbands seemed to have a close rapport with her daughter-in-law, and she explained that the code of conjugal rotation that the men follow with their wife maintains harmony in the household.

We also went to visit the chimi, Tashi Wangdi, who represents Merak and Sakteng in Bhutan's National Assembly. He is one of the wealthiest men in the village, and the shrine room in his house boasts an exquisitely carved altar filled with gilded Buddha images.

The next stop was the house of the gup (the village headman), who was once the reputed strongman of Merak, famous for being able to lift a young bull yak and place it on his back. He attempted this feat in our presence, but was clearly past his prime—the yak pranced away and the gup was left sheepishly holding a hunk of yak hair in his hand. The gup had organized an evening of typical Merak entertainment for us on the spacious top floor of his house. There was singing and dancing, and copious amounts of ara were drunk. Everyone got jollier as the evening progressed, and the women decided to bestow their special blessings on our host. Five of them pinned him down, and poured ara on his face and pelted him with popcorn which stuck to his wet hair—the second time in the day that the gup was left looking sheepish.

In the course of that merry evening, I learned much about the way of life of the Brokpas. When frost begins to cover the pastures where their yaks graze, many of the Brokpas, in Merak as well as Sakteng, close up their houses and descend to the lower regions of Tashigang district to trade with the villagers there. A unique relationship, known as Drukor, has developed between the Brokpas and the lowland villagers—in a tradition going back centuries, most Brokpa families have a 'host family' or Nepo in the lowland villages, with whom they have a close trading as well as social relationship. They stay in their Nepo's house for weeks, eat and sleep there like members of his family, and leave butter and cheese for him to barter in exchange for grain and maize. The Nepo in turn, comes up to Sakteng and Merak to stay with his Brokpa family in summer, bringing grain, vegetables and fruit.

I learned too about their annual Jomo Kora festival, in honour of Aum Jomo. The Brokpas believe that Aum Jomo's heavenly home is on the mountain of Jomo Kukhar, about a seven- or eight-hour walk south of Merak. Every autumn, the people of Merak make a pilgrimage to this mountain, to seek her blessings for their health and prosperity. It is a two-day festival, and there is much merriment as they make the day-long trek to the base of the mountain. There are horse races as the men ride up, and anyone whose cap falls off or belt comes untied during the trek is 'fined' a bottle of ara. In the evening they reach the foot of Aum Jomo's mountain and spend the night there, wrapped in their heavy yak-wool blankets. Early the next morning, a great ritual prayer is held at the foot of the mountain, after which the men climb up to the summit—women who have attained puberty are not allowed to set foot on the mountain lest they pollute Aum Jomo's holy abode. After more prayers at the summit, from where the plains of Assam and West Bengal can be seen on a clear day, everyone returns to Merak, for a day of feasting, dancing and drinking. All the ara that has been collected as 'fines' is consumed!

Throughout this tour I had noticed that the houses of the Brokpas, with their tiny windows to keep out the cold, were filled with smoke from the stoves—it was no wonder that respiratory complaints were the main health problem in both Sakteng and Merak. The district government has wisely involved gomchens (lay monks) in their public health and nutrition campaigns and projects in the region. Gomchens—of whom there are a particularly large number in eastern Bhutan—are married, and follow farming and other occupations, yet have the religious training to conduct rituals and prayers. This makes them extremely influential in their communities, and thus very effective as agents of social change.

My companions on this tour to Merak and Sakteng included health, agriculture and veterinary experts and, between us, we carried vaccines and medicines for humans and animals, high-altitude seeds for kitchen gardens and newly designed labour-saving spindles and butter churners. I had also brought with me iceboxes for each household in Merak and Sakteng, for transporting their yak butter and cheese to Tashigang and Thimphu—these were the biggest hit! And I took back with me a treasured gift, a beautiful Brokpa costume complete with tsipee cham cap, which I keep carefully in a chest at my home in Thimphu. No doubt in a few years' time there will be a motorable road almost all the way to Sakteng and Merak, which will certainly bring more ease and prosperity into the lives of the Brokpas. But I would be surprised if it changed their culture and traditions in any fundamental way. Like the yak-herding communities of Laya and Lunana, the Brokpas deeply value the freedom of their way of life. They love the rugged grandeur of their land and would not easily exchange these for the tamer pleasures—and stresses—of life in Tashigang or Thimphu.

I cannot end this account of my visit to Sakteng and Merak without saying something about the Yeti, or Abominable Snowman, for while I was there I heard many stories about this elusive creature. Most Yeti encounters are related by yak herders, who spend much of their time in isolated areas at high altitudes, grazing their yaks, or in dense forests, searching for animals who have strayed. They are also the ones who most often encounter that other elusive creature, the snow leopard which, of course, we know for a fact exists. The Brokpa name for the Yeti is Megay. Some say their coat is reddish grey, others that it is white. But all accounts agree that the creature is about seven feet tall, its footprints are about a foot long, the distance between each footprint is four feet, and it emits a strong, distinctive odour. Brokpa tradition, instilled even in children, maintains that should one see a Yeti it should be treated with the utmost respect and reverence, for it is a guardian deity of these remote areas, and does not attack human beings unless provoked. And if it is provoked or attacked, it will kill mercilessly and bring catastrophe on the entire community.

About a month after I had left the land of the Brokpas, in June–July 2001, the dungpa (administrator) of Merak and Sakteng, Tashi Darge, along with three other men, went on a quest for the Yeti. It was the season when the fresh bamboo shoots sprout and the Yeti is believed to be especially partial to this delicacy. Tashi Darge's group took dry rations with them, not wanting to light a fire and thus alert the Yeti. When they reached a place called Mereksemo, near the pass between Sakteng and Merak, they saw footprints that were about a foot long. An overpowering odour, rather like that of the allium or wild highland garlic—another favourite food of the Yeti—permeated the surroundings. The footprints led towards a cave in a cliff, deep in the forest, which they reached with great difficulty. On a tree near the cave, at the height of about seven feet, they found some reddish fur, where the creature must have rubbed itself. And near a corner of the cave they found excrement with evidence of bamboo shoots and allium. Tashi Darge took photographs of the footprints, made moulds of them in plaster of Paris, and collected samples of the hair, which they submitted to the government. These were then sent to a reputed scientific institution to be analysed. The report stated that the hair did not belong to any known species. We continue to hear credible reports of Yeti sightings from Merak and Sakteng, and from another district in eastern Bhutan, Tashi Yangtse. Surveillance cameras have been left in likely habitats. But so far, the creature has continued to elude us.

CHAPTER 14

BULLS WITH BLAZING HORNS
AND OTHER VIGNETTES

Every time I travel within Bhutan, I am struck anew by the extraordinary variety of peoples and ways of life that flourish in our small country. Such is the lay of the land that often there is no contact at all between villages that may be just a few kilometres apart as the crow flies, but are completely cut off from each other by high mountains and deep gorges. Physical inaccessibility has created isolated pockets of habitation, sealed off from any outside influences, which have preserved intact over the centuries their very distinctive cultures.

In my travels into the interiors of the districts of Chukha, Samtse and Tongsa, I encountered for the first time ethnic groups and languages, customs and practices that even most Bhutanese do not know of. My experiences travelling on foot through the south-western districts of Dagana and Tsirang were special for different reasons. I did not tell the district officials that I was coming, and during this tour I spent several nights in village homes, without any fuss or formality. I shared the villagers' hearth and home like a member of the family, and this certainly deepened my understanding of their attitudes and perceptions, and the hardships and problems they face. It also led to encounters with some remarkable people with whom, through the Tarayana Foundation, I have formed lifelong associations. This chapter is a mosaic, made up of vignettes from my travels in these five districts.

One does not always have to travel long distances on foot to discover hidden treasures or see extraordinary sights in Bhutan. In a little village, a four-hour drive south of Thimphu, on the Thimphu–Phuentsoling Highway, I witnessed a centuries-old practice which is not just unique to this particular hamlet but perhaps the world over. Merisemo is a village of fifty-eight households, which I had wanted to visit ever since I read the vivid descriptions of it in the accounts of Captain Samuel Turner, who travelled to Bhutan in 1783, as an envoy of Warren Hastings, the British Governor General in Calcutta.

If there is a place that epitomizes Timeless Bhutan, it is Merisemo, for it is still almost exactly as Turner had described it more than 200 years ago. Turner was awestruck by the scenery as he approached Merisemo (he calls it Murichom), which fell on his route as he made the tortuous journey from the foothills bordering the Bengal–Bhutan border, up to Thimphu:

> At every pause we beheld a different prospect, each of which, perhaps, might justly be reckoned amongst the grandest and most awful in nature. Cascades of water issuing from the bosoms of lofty mountains, clothed with noble trees, and hiding their heads in the clouds; abrupt precipices, deep dells, and the river dashing its waters with astonishing rapidity over the huge stones and broken rocks below, composed the sublime and variegated picture.

The route that Turner took was one I knew well from my childhood journeys to my boarding school in India, when every feature of this majestic landscape became familiar to me. Fortunately, I didn't have to do this journey on foot, as my father did when he made his annual trip with his mules to Kalimpong. In those days, the only way to cross a deep gorge over the Chukha river was over a notoriously precarious rope bridge near Merisemo, and Turner provides a graphic account of the experience:

> It consisted of two large ropes made of twisted creepers, stretched parallel to each other and encircled with a hoop. The traveller has only to place himself between the ropes, and sit down on the hoop, seizing one rope in each hand, by means of which he slides himself along, and crosses an abyss on which I could not look without shuddering.

This particular rope bridge is now gone, but there are many others like it elsewhere in rural Bhutan—I've never had the courage to use them!

The houses at Merisemo, as in most villages in western Bhutan, are even today just as Turner described them: built of stone and clay, the walls narrowing from the foundations to the top, the gently pitched shingle roof supported clear of the walls, with large stones to weight it down, and the space between the roof and the top floor used to store firewood and grain. The rooms are large, with floors made of wood; the staircase is a log of wood with notches cut into it. Projecting balconies on the top floor provide light and space, and a pleasant space for the women to sit and weave. Turner's observant eye even noticed how the doors turn on pivots, without the use of metal hinges or nails. The only change since Turner's visit is that the animals at Merisemo are no longer kept on the ground floor, but in pens on the outskirts of the village. The wild strawberries, raspberries and peach trees that he wrote about still grow in abundance. And the ficus tree that Turner planted has grown enormous, and dominates the centre of Merisemo.

Today, as in Turner's day, the most striking feature of Merisemo is its beautifully terraced fields gently rising up the mountainside. Turner admiringly noted the skill with which the terracing was done, but he did not discover the most extraordinary farming method practised by the villagers there. Merisemo's terraced paddy fields are not fed by any irrigation channel and are totally dependent on rainfall. When the rains begin, and the planting season starts, the villagers of Merisemo work at this laborious task through the nights to make the most of the rainfall. And how do they manage to do this work, which requires great precision and care, in the pitch-black darkness of the night? By tying flaming branches of resinous pine to the horns of their bulls! It is one of the most magical sights you can imagine—the blazing horns moving like twinkling stars in the night, casting a gentle golden glow over the tender, green paddy shoots, the tiered amphitheatre of fields and the colourful kiras of the women, singing through the night as they bend over the seedlings, calf-deep in rainwater.

Another famous feature of Merisemo that Turner missed is its sacred cave, sanctified by the Goddess of Long Life, Tseringma—a deep limestone cavern with stalactites and stalagmites covering the floor and hanging from the roof. The cave was wet and slippery that day, so I couldn't explore it fully, but the villagers told me that, further in, the cave floor drops deep into the earth and leads to an underground lake.

My visit to Merisemo and its neighbouring hamlets was memorable also for the people I met. In Kethokha, the village across the valley from Merisemo, I encountered a sixty-nine-year-old woman, Aum Tandin Om, renowned as a clairvoyant. Dancing and chanting, with a torma (ritual sculpture made of butter and rice) balanced on her head, the old lady went into a trance and then began to speak: 'I see our King going into battle, with his vision clearer than a mirror. I see Genyen Jampa Melay [the Protecting Deity of the Thimphu Valley] in armour accompanying our King. The battle will end in a great victory.' I didn't realize at the time that she was foretelling with uncanny accuracy events that would take place more than two years later, about which I have written in Chapter 8. Another person I remember from this tour was the National Assembly member from the area, a thin, dark and taciturn elderly man—a most unlikely-looking Lothario, who had a wife in every village in his territory. Apart from bringing romance and excitement to his life, this ensured that he regularly made rounds of all the villages and so kept himself closely informed about local events and problems. The wife in Kethokha was in her twenties, with a baby strapped to her back. Not long after we met him, he died in a car accident, leaving a string of widows of varying ages, from teenagers to fifty-year-olds.

The Lhops of south-western Bhutan and the Monpas of central Bhutan are two distinct ethnic groups, who retain their own languages and cultures, and have remained relatively untouched by the modern world. During my visits to the Lhop and Monpa settlements I was able to observe their lives at close quarters, and my long talks with the elders in these communities yielded much fascinating information, which I hope will provide new areas of research for anthropologists.

The Lhop settlements lie beyond the Chamurchi river in Samtse district, in the Amochhu river valley. Oranges and cardamom are the major cash crops in this region, and in the orange-harvesting season, the Lhops emerge from their villages to work as porters. Barefoot and bare-shouldered, the Lhops stand out in their homespun white cotton tunics, crossed over their chest and knotted at the shoulder, as they carry baskets of oranges down to the auction yard in the town of Samtse.

When I set off to visit their settlements, in February 2001—the tail end of the orange-harvesting season—I had to cross the Chamurchi river no less than twenty-four times. To save ourselves the trouble of taking off and putting on our shoes twenty-four times, my companions and I decided to trek in plastic slippers. They gave us all terrible blisters between the toes, and made a hideous *tep-tep* sound as we limped along in them—no wonder the Bhutanese word for plastic slippers is *teytem*.

The river crossings behind us, the next hurdle was crossing the Yebila Pass, a strenuous climb during which all of us grumbled, until we encountered a stream of porters, including a sixty-year-old woman, stoically carrying their heavy loads over the pass. I sank down to rest under a lush canopy of trees around a rock pool, an enchanting spot, where the porters stopped to drink water and chat

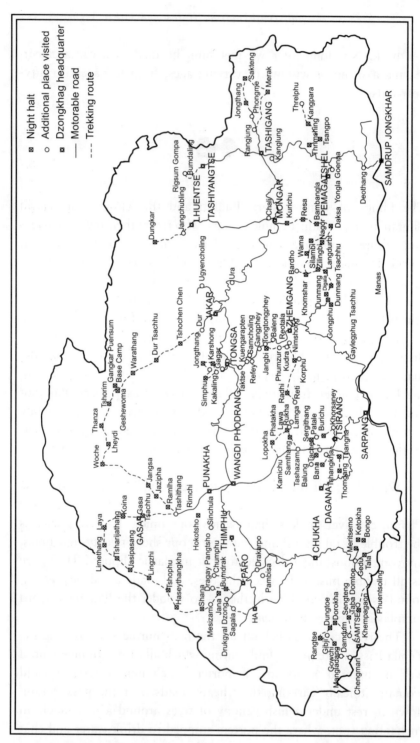

Remote areas visited by the author

with us. I took out a statue that I always carry with me—an image of Goddess Tseringma and her four sisters and their teacher, the saint Milarepa, carved on rhino horn. It was a moving experience to see each porter bend his weary head to touch it to the statue and receive the blessings of the goddess.

I spent that night in pouring rain, at Sengteng village, where the inhabitants are predominantly Rais, a caste of the Lhotsampa community, who were originally from Nepal and have made their home in this corner of Bhutan. That evening, I witnessed a ritual performed by Birkha Bahadur Rai, fifty-six, a Jakri (shaman), who with great solemnity prepared an offering consisting of one raw egg, three pieces of ginger, yeast water and nine different plants. He lit a lamp, beat a deafening tattoo on aluminium plates, offered water in four directions and then pronounced his predictions—which was that the future looked too hazy to predict with any certainty! At any rate it was a splendid show.

The next morning, I met the assembled village community, distributed vegetable seeds to bring some variety and better nutrition to their diet, and invited them to tell me about their problems and to ask questions. One man got up and said he had a question: 'Just who are you?' he asked in genuine puzzlement. The entire assembly burst into laughter, and this completely broke the ice. This question— a very fundamental one, after all—was probably the best question I've ever been asked during my tours of rural Bhutan! Indeed, on this trip, it was I who asked the stupidest question—passing fields of fern-like plants I wondered aloud what they were. The villagers walking with me looked incredulous as they informed me that these were cardamom plants! No doubt to help me get over my embarrassment, they told me about a foreign agricultural expert who had come here some years earlier—he thought cardamom grew on trees. And then there is the well-known (and true) story about the yak expert who came to Bhutan under the auspices of an international organization and asked what that strange hairy beast was the first time he actually saw a real live yak!

The next morning, I walked from Sengteng to Lotokuchu, a large settlement of Lhops, who live in a world so very different from that of the Rais. The Lhops' houses are on two-foot-high stilts, made of wood and bamboo, with thatched roofs. I noticed strange piles of stones around their houses. Apart from their distinctive clothes, the Lhops also stand out because of their diminutive size—their height ranges from four feet to five feet. Nevertheless they are sturdy and extremely agile, able to clamber up trees and steep cliffs in search of fodder for their cattle or reeds with which to thatch their houses. They are also skilled archers, and reputed to make the best bows in Bhutan from the bamboo that grows near their settlements.

Little is known about the origin of the Lhops, but their oral tradition suggests that they were originally semi-nomadic herders who lived in the foothills and were then forced further into the interior by later migrants. Their legends also indicate that they were originally a much larger group, but were decimated by smallpox and by feuds between their own clans, sometime in the seventeenth and eighteenth centuries. Consanguinity is common among the Lhops and this may be a reason for their short stature, as well as for the high incidence of cretinism among them.

The Lhops' religion is largely animist. Their deities, who live in rocks, caves, mountains, waterfalls and lakes, are appeased by sacrificing pigs and roosters. One common ritual involves cutting off the head of a rooster and placing the decapitated head on the rooftop, with its head turned towards the source of the Amochhu river. If a cat, eagle or crow disturbs or carries away the rooster's head it is regarded as a bad omen for that household.

The Lhops' funeral rites are unlike any I have heard of. They do not cremate their dead, but bury them above the ground in wooden coffins together with their belongings (such as clothes, shoes, ornaments and cups). They then cover the coffins with great mounds of stone. Each dead person is formally assigned a piece of land. Then a bull is sacrificed if the deceased is a male, and a cow if it is a female. The entire community is invited for a feast and the meat divided among them. The spirit of the dead person is then solemnly invoked, and beseeched to leave the family in peace. The verse, chanted in chorus, says: 'We are giving you your share of grains, property, livestock. Take them, and make offerings to the deities for the safe journey of your soul. Do not trouble us any more, we are giving you your share.'

The Lhops speak a language called Ngentam, which has over the years assimilated a number of Dzongkha words, but spoken in such a different accent that I couldn't understand a single word. The head of a Lhop family is the maternal uncle, who is known as the *Ku*. He assigns each member of the family their tasks, is responsible for their welfare and settles disputes. Even after the Ku marries and has his own family, he continues to be the head of his sisters' families. If a Lhop's husband or wife dies of unnatural causes, the widow or widower does not remarry or cut their hair for nine years.

After meeting the eighty-three households of Lotokuchu, I continued on foot, spending another three nights en route at scattered Lhop settlements. I met a frail and elderly Lhop couple who had no children, and the Tarayana Foundation has now adopted them. We give them an annual stipend and take care of their medical needs. Everywhere, I was impressed by the gentle ways of the Lhops, and their great pride in their tribal identity and distinctive culture. I realized anew how important it is to respect, preserve and record their way of life, which is an integral part of Bhutan's cultural heritage, and to ensure that their participation in the progress and development taking place elsewhere in the country is at their own pace and on their own terms. This was a conviction that was reinforced when I visited the Monpa settlements in Tongsa district, a year later.

The three main Monpa villages, Jangbi, Wangling and Phumzur, with a population of 260, are in the buffer zone of the Jigme Singye Wangchuck National Park, in central Bhutan. Believed to be the oldest original inhabitants of Bhutan, the Monpas have their own language, Monkha, which is quite different from any other language or dialect spoken in Bhutan, though it has its roots in the Tibeto-Burman family of languages. They also have their own religion, and worship local spirits who dwell in sacred groves, mountains, rocks, cliffs, rivers, the wind and the sky. The highest peak in the region,

Mt Jow Durshing, is their sacred mountain which they believe marks the centre of the earth. Until a few years ago animal sacrifice was quite prevalent among the Monpas, but now they have been persuaded by the lamas of Tongsa to use animals sculpted from wheat dough for their rituals. The Monpas are almost entirely dependent on the forests which surround their villages for their livelihood and their daily needs. Their knowledge and management of forest resources, including medicinal herbs, is unsurpassed, as are their conservation practices which ensure that these continue to regenerate. On my visit to the Monpa villages, I was fortunate to have as my guide and interpreter a respected elder of the Monpa community, Ap Tawla.

I embarked on this three-week tour after spending the night at the guest house above Tongsa Dzong. This enormous dzong, perched high on the cliffs above the Mangdechhu river, is one of the wonders of Bhutan. Driving from Thimphu to Tongsa on the East–West Highway, the dzong suddenly comes into view as one turns a corner. For the next 14 kilometres, as the road winds like a corkscrew along the mountainside, the dzong appears and disappears, presenting a different aspect of its magnificent architecture each time. In autumn, this is a particularly scenic drive with the pink blossoms of the wild cherry trees adding vivid splashes of colour.

Built in 1644, Tongsa Dzong has always been of great strategic and historic importance. In the old days before the motor road was built, the mule track to eastern Bhutan passed right through the dzong, so whoever controlled this dzong also controlled all east–west traffic and trade. The father of Bhutan's first king was the powerful Penlop (governor) of Tongsa Dzong, and since then his descendants have been the hereditary Penlops of Tongsa. The present King became the fifteenth Penlop of Tongsa at the age of fifteen, and the present Crown Prince was invested with this title in 2004. As one enters the dzong, which is vast and rambling, one feels that one has entered a medieval town—its winding corridors which are as wide as streets, lead to staircases, courtyards, palaces and no less than 24 beautiful temples, built at different levels along the hillside.

From Tongsa Dzong I continued on the motor road for about

50 kilometres, before beginning my journey on foot. Crossing the suspension bridge over the Mangdechhu river, I began the gentle walk to Monpa country. It took us just two hours to reach Jangbi, the first Monpa village, but it seemed I had travelled several centuries back in time.

The Monpa houses are small and simple, with wooden floors and support beams, the walls made of bamboo matting reinforced with mud plaster, and the roof thatched with dried banana leaf or bamboo matting. Over the next few days I tried to learn a few phrases of the musical Monpa language—'*Gur-ma-gur, chat-ma-chat*' means peace and happiness, which sort of summed up my mood as I spent three days in their company. I saw only a few of the older generation wearing the traditional Monpa dress called *pagay*, a sleeveless tunic. It is woven of fibre made from nettle plants, rough but extremely durable. Sadly, only a handful of women today know how to weave this nettle cloth—the Monpas now prefer wearing kiras and ghos which they buy in Tongsa. I met ten traditional healers in the three villages—the Monpas still prefer to be treated by them, though there is a Basic Health Unit in the area. Ap Tawla told me their medicines are made from thirty-four different species of plants found in the forest, and their knowledge of herbal medicine is still meticulously passed down from generation to generation.

The food I ate with the Monpas were feasts fit for the gods. Apart from the maize, millet and rice they grow in their fields, almost everything else they eat is gathered from the forest. The Monpas offer the first crops from their harvest to their deities, in thirty-two bamboo cups. Ap Tawla told me they eat ten kinds of wild fruit, six kinds of fern, ten kinds of mushroom, tender shoots of cane and bamboo, wild tubers and orchid buds. They brew tea from the leaves of fifteen different plants, make the most fragrant incense from six plants, and vegetable dyes from a number of leaves, roots and bark. Their cooking oil comes from the fruit and seeds of ten different plants, the most prized of which is the yikashing (*Aesandra butyracea*) tree. It has an olive-sized pinkish fruit—I'm toying with the idea of promoting extra-virgin cold-pressed yikashing oil as the next big must-have for celebrity chefs and foodies in New York.

The main source of livelihood for the Monpas is their skill in making objects of bamboo and cane. At Jangbi village I saw an exhibition of these crafts—beautiful traditional baskets, hats and mats, as well as a few chairs, tables and picture frames they had started making after some of them were sent on a study tour to Assam, in north-east India. These should find an excellent market in Bhutan's urban centres. Hand in hand with the Monpas' close dependence on the forest goes their care in ensuring that forest resources are never depleted. Monpa tradition has designated several forest areas as sacred groves, where absolutely nothing can be touched. They also have their own community-enforced rules— gathering cane and bamboo is restricted only to certain seasons, and harvesting young shoots is prohibited. Such rules ensure that every plant or tree they use continues to regenerate.

In every Monpa village, people told me they want roads, electricity and telephones. I have no doubt that in a few years' time these will come, for they are close enough to the motor road to make this viable. It is inevitable that the Monpas will increasingly be influenced by mainstream society, for theirs is a vibrant and living culture, not an exhibit in a museum diorama. But I hope they never lose their understanding and appreciation of their environment, their wealth of knowledge of forest resources, from which the rest of the country has so much to learn.

The Monpas are a matriarchal community. Marriages between first cousins are common, and their marriage customs are unique. When a young couple decides to get married, the boy goes to live in the girl's house, works in her family's fields and contributes to their earnings. After three years the girl's parents send an emissary to the boy's family to convey the following message: 'Your son is in my house, his eyes are not blind, his legs and arms are not broken, do you need him back?' If they say no, the boy stays on in his wife's house, but if his parents want him back, they send a formal apology and gifts to the bride's house, and the young couple then move into the husband's house. There, his parents transfer all their property to their daughter-in-law, as an assurance that her husband will not abandon her. But if he does, it is he who must leave the house, and his wife retains all his family's assets. She can even remarry and bring her new husband to the house.

Apart from their own deities, the Monpas also revere Guru Padmasambhava, who came to this region in the eighth century. My Monpa companions pointed out many rocks with the foot- and handprints of the Guru. From Phumzur, the last of the three Monpa villages I visited, it was an eight-hour trek to Kubdra, where I saw the ruins of the palace of the ancient Monpa king, Marapai, who hosted the Guru when he travelled through this region. I spent the night there and the next day walked six hours to Nabji, an important historic site, associated with the Guru. In the middle of a beautiful stretch of paddy fields, which have been cultivated continuously for over thirteen centuries, stands a tiny temple in the shade of a towering cypress tree. At the centre of the temple is a stone pillar with the thumbprints of the Guru, and the two warring kings, Sendha Gyab (also known as Sindhu Raja) and Nowache, whose long-running battles had caused so much bloodshed. The Guru persuaded the two kings to meet at this place, take an oath to make peace forever, and seal that promise with their thumbprints on this pillar. I felt very privileged to have seen this pillar of peace with its great historic and religious associations.

After visiting the Monpa villages, I continued my tour of all the remaining gewogs (counties) in Tongsa district, and came upon an extraordinary sight in the middle of the Jigme Singye Wangchuck National Park. Crossing the Dhungkala (Conch Shell) Pass, I was amazed to find a paved road running for 21 kilometres through the forest, leading to Gongkhola. Here in the 1970s, the Geological Survey of India (at that time Bhutan did not have its own department of geology) had discovered copper. The estimated reserve in this area was 2.5 million tonnes of copper at every 100 metres of vertical depth. The Gongkhola Copper Exploitation project was launched in 1978-79. And now, in 2002, I saw a ghost town, where time had stood still. I saw barracks covered in tattered tarpaulin, an office with a 3D model of the mountains with the drilling sites marked on it, boxes and boxes of tubes and pipes, a signal office, a guest house, a hospital, a canteen, a cinema hall where a new movie would be airdropped once a week; houses for mining officials and their families, a jeep and a truck rusting in a shed. With the exception of a lone caretaker, the whole place was deserted, abandoned and very,

very eerie. A couple of years into the project, the Government of Bhutan decided to stop the prospecting, forgo the copper and preserve the rich biodiversity of this National Park. It was a decision that must have gladdened the hearts of the Monpas and their deities and spirits who dwell in these mountains.

It was 4 o'clock in the morning. The raucous crowing of a rooster jerked me out of a deep sleep and, as my eyes adjusted to the dark, I remembered where I was—in a little alcove off the kitchen of a farmhouse in Tachchey village, in Dagana district. This was Aum Dema's house, where I had spent the night after a hard day's walk in the hot sun, through paddy fields and forests and over rocky hills. Around me in the large kitchen, which was also the family common room, lay the huddled sleeping figures of three generations of Aum Dema's family. The warmth from the earthen stove, on which we had cooked our dinner together the night before, still lingered. Leading off from the kitchen was the prayer room, with its magnificently carved and painted altar, and seven bowls of water in front of gilded images of the Buddha, Guru Padmasambhava and Zhabdrung Ngawang Namgyel. Tiptoeing in the dark, I placed the gift I had brought for Aum Dema on her altar—three butter lamps—and prayed that my hostess would always be prosperous enough to fill them with butter. Outside in the courtyard, I could see the silhouette of a magnificent peach tree laden with blossom. Aum Dema's home brought back nostalgic memories of my childhood home in Nobgang, with its peach and apple trees, and the closeness of family ties between the three generations of our own family who lived together. I quietly made my way to the outdoor toilet before the early morning darkness lifted, for with the first light the whole family would be up. Their waking, working and sleeping hours were dictated by the progress of the sun across the sky, as Tachchey, like most villages in the interior of Dagana, had no electricity. Aum Dema's two-storeyed house was black with the soot from pine resin, the only source of warmth and light in the house.

In the spring of 2004, I set off on a ten-day tour of villages in Dagana and Tsirang, two districts in south-western Bhutan. This time, since my tour was planned without the knowledge of district officials, I would not camp in a tent, but would eat and sleep in village houses, or in a sleeping bag under the starry skies. I would carry my own backpack, walk at my own pace, and meet and talk to people in a completely unplanned and spontaneous way.

In Dagana, as elsewhere in remote rural areas, I learned that what the villagers wanted most of all was electricity and better access to a motor road. Where villages are large and the houses clustered close together, building roads and bringing electricity is viable, as in my own village, Nobgang. But here in Dagana, there were no big villages, and the houses were scattered at a considerable distance from each other. The King had proposed a resettlement scheme, where people could move to planned habitations at lower altitudes with all the modern conveniences provided and with easy access to the motor road, but here, as in the remote villages of Kheng, the scheme found few takers—people were too attached to their ancestral land and homes.

One morning, as we sat under a large cypress tree in Balung village, where the villagers usually held their meetings, we discussed this problem at length. Eventually a solution came to me—the Tarayana Foundation would provide solar panels and solar lanterns to these households. As I write this a year later, there is light in the evenings in Aum Dema's house and in the other villages I visited— for the women to weave and the children to study, the men to do carpentry and repair their agricultural tools, and for neighbours to visit each other. Providing solar panels to these villages has been one of the most satisfying projects taken up by the Tarayana Foundation.

Whenever I visit village houses, people like to show me their treasures—a holy relic, or heirloom jewellery, or a fine kira they have woven. Here at Balung, Ran Maya held out her treasure for me to admire—her ten-year-old daughter Phool Maya, who was stricken with spina bifida. The child's upper torso was crumpled, and her legs twined around her mother's waist. Handicapped children are often hidden away when guests come, but Ran Maya's look of pride and adoration as she introduced her daughter moved me deeply.

Phool Maya has been adopted by the Tarayana Foundation, and we hope surgery and physiotherapy will eventually enable her to lead a more independent life. At another Dagana village, Zinchela, I met fourteen-year-old Purni Maya, whose hands were webbed like a duck's feet. Despite this handicap, she displayed tremendous spirit, demonstrating to me how well she could write and draw. I was struck by her intelligence, too, and her hunger for education. Our foundation now sponsors her education and her daily needs, and I have a feeling Purni Maya will go far in life.

Not all my experiences in Dagana were as heart-warming. There were houses I went to where the women were alcoholics and their children neglected. And though there are well-equipped Basic Health Units accessible from every village, I found that far too many sick people simply do not go to them. Dorji, the headman of Lajab gewog, who joined me on part of the tour, took me through beautiful forests to his village. His wife had been ill for two years now, and the village seer convinced him that her illness was caused by an evil spirit in his house. So Dorji had demolished his beautiful old house, and was now in the process of constructing a new one, at the edge of his paddy fields. I was impressed by his devotion to his wife, but dismayed at the senseless destruction, and the waste of his hard-earned money.

I also learned that the location of schools and Basic Health Units was the cause of much discord between villages in Dagana. The villagers of Balung and the next village, Phuensumgang, for example, could not reach a consensus on where the school should be located. The usual practice in rural Bhutan is that the children from neighbouring villages are housed and fed by families in the village where the school is located. But in this case, both villages, having failed to reach an agreement, took a dog-in-the-manger attitude. The school was then built in no-man's-land, which meant people from both villages had to build little shacks around the school where a family member or parent lived with the schoolgoing children, cooking and looking after them. I had noticed similar feuds between neighbouring villages in Tongsa district. Perhaps it would be best to decide the location of schools and health units by lottery, or the toss of a coin.

By the time I finished my tour of Dagana, I had deep blisters on my feet from the hours of walking this steep and rocky terrain, and I was covered with bites from the sandflies (we call them *damdim*) that infest this area. (Captain William Turner too had suffered the bites of this horrible little fly, which he first encountered in Merisemo. 'It is exceedingly irritating and troublesome,' he wrote, 'a severe tax upon so delightful a place as Murichom, which by nature is one of the most beautiful I have seen.') I rested for a day at Dagana Dzong to get my bites and blisters treated, before driving for three hours to reach Damphu, the capital of Tsirang district. The town is perched on top of a ridge, with spectacular views of the countryside around it—the terrain I would walk through for the next four days.

The exquisite scent of orange blossom filled the air as I began walking the next morning, for Tsirang is dotted with orange orchards on both sides of the valley. The land here is fertile, far less steep and rocky than in Dagana, and the footpaths are wide and well maintained. We passed through the idyllic villages of Khorsanigaon and Phentechu, stopping for tea at the home of a Gurung family— an impeccably clean two-storey mud house—and ending the day at Dhan Maya's house, where the villagers put on an impromptu show. Both Dagana and Tsirang have a large population of Lhotsampas, who migrated to these parts from their original homes in Nepal and the Darjeeling Hills of India. They are hard-working and skilled cultivators, whose fields and orange groves are beautifully tended. The evening at Dhan Maya's house was a delightful interlude, where we sat in her garden lit by the gentle light of lanterns, discovered the incomparable taste of oranges straight off the tree, and enjoyed the lilting songs and rhythmic dances of the Lhotsampas.

At the next village, Tsirangtoe, I met ninety-seven-year-old Ranmaya Rai, an alert and still active lady, cherished and revered by the entire village. Behind the Tsirangtoe school I came upon the ruins of an enormous fort, its massive stone outer walls, crumbling stairways and imposing gateway overgrown with vegetation. Nobody in the village could tell me anything about it, or why it had fallen into ruin, except that it dated to the Zhabdrung's time, the mid-seventeenth century. Villagers ploughing the field around the ruins had come upon old coins and zees, but had promptly put them back into the earth for fear that they might bring bad luck. The zee, a rare agate with circular shapes known as 'eyes' on it, is the most valued gemstone for the Bhutanese, worn as a good-luck charm on a string of coral beads. Maybe the 'eyes' were naturally formed, or etched on the agate by a technique that is now lost, but the price of zees has risen astronomically, the most valuable ones being those with the most 'eyes'. It seems there is buried treasure worth millions of ngultrums lying beneath the fields and forests of Tsirangtoe.

Over the next two days I walked through the villages and orange groves of Patala and Sergethang, At Sergethang, I met four-year-old Kinlay Zam, a sad-eyed child whose mother had died and her father had gone back to his village in faraway Sakteng. The Tarayana Foundation now sends an annual stipend to the little girl's grandmother for her clothes and schoolbooks. From here, a hard day's trek brought me to the road-head at Burichu, where my car was waiting.

This trip had opened my eyes to a major problem facing the people living in these idyllic orange-scented villages. With no easy access to the motor road, there was no market for their beautiful oranges, they told me—the sad irony is that it costs far more to transport their oranges to urban markets than to grow them. Our Foundation doesn't have the resources to build the roads they need—in any case, that is the responsibility of the government—but we now lobby actively for the needs of the orange growers of Tsirang, whose livelihoods will be transformed by better access to roads.

On the altar in my shrine room at home is a stone shaped like a chorten, given to me by an old lady in a village in Tongsa. She had found it in a riverbed and kept it on her own altar until the day I walked into her home. Buffeted and sculpted by ice and snow, rocks and water, on its long journey down from the Himalayas to a village in the heart of Bhutan, that stone is for me a symbol of the journeys I have made. And locked inside it, like treasures sealed in a chorten, are the seeds of journeys still to come—there are so many treasures of the Thunder Dragon that still wait to be discovered.

GLOSSARY

Anim: nun

Ap: respectful term of address for an older man

Ara: distilled alcohol made from grain

Ashang: Uncle

Ashi: title given to women of the royal family

Atsara: jesters or clowns who perform during a tsechu

Aum: term of address for a married woman

Bangchu: round, lidded cane basket

Beyul: hidden places scattered throughout the Himalayas, chosen by Guru Padmasambhava to serve as places of refuge for the people and their religion, in times of trouble and turmoil

Bodhisattva: enlightened beings in Mahayana Buddhism who are able to reach nirvana but defer it so that they can devote themselves to the service of others

Bon: Religion with shamanistic and animist practices that predated Buddhism in the Himalayan region

Brokpas: inhabitants of the valleys of Merak and Sakteng in eastern Bhutan

Chenrezig: the Bodhisattva of Compassion, also known as Avalokiteswara

Chhu: river or water

Chimi: member of Bhutan's National Assembly

Choku: religious ceremony or puja

Chorten: religious structure, also known as stupa, usually containing sacred relics

Chugo: hard, dried cheese

Chungkay: fermented rice porridge cooked with butter and eggs

Dapa: lustrous wooden bowl or cup; the most prized ones are usually made from the knotty burr of a maple tree.

Dasho: a title given by the king to senior officials. A Dasho wears a red scarf.

Datse: traditional archery, the most popular sport in Bhutan

Desi Tenzin Rabgye (1638–96): Fourth temporal ruler of Bhutan

Desi: title given to the temporal ruler of Bhutan from 1851 to 1905; known as the Deb Raja in British colonial accounts

Deysi: sweet saffron rice

Dochey: inner courtyard of a dzong

Doma: areca nut wrapped in betel leaf and lime paste

Domchoe: annual religious festival held at Punakha and Thimphu Dzongs, dedicated to the Protecting Deities of Bhutan, instituted by Zhabdrung Ngawang Namgyel

Dorji Phagmo: powerful goddess in Tantric Mahayana Buddhism

Dorji: double thunderbolt symbol, which represents the purity and wisdom that brings enlightenment

Druk Gyalpo: formal title held by the ruler of Bhutan

Druk Yul: Land of the Thunder Dragon, the name for Bhutan in Dzongkha

Druk: thunder dragon

Drukpa Kargyupa: the sect of Buddhism that is the official state religion of Bhutan

Drukpa Kinlay (1455–1529): saint of the Drukpa Kargyupa school, who spread his teachings through unorthodox methods; also known as the 'Divine Madman'

Drupchen: annual prayers held in a temple

Duar: Indian word meaning doorway or gate, which refers to the traditional entrances to Bhutan from the Bengal and Assam plains of India

Dungpa: administrator of a sub-district

Dungtsho: doctor of traditional medicine

Dzong: fortress-like structure in Bhutan that usually houses administrative offices as well as the monk body

Dzongda: administrative head of a district

Dzongkha: the official language of Bhutan (literally, language spoken in the dzong)

Dzongkhag: district

Ema datsi: dish of chillies cooked with cheese

Ezay: a chutney or relish made with chillies

Gang: hill

Gelong: ordained monk

Gewog: county, consisting of a block of villages

Gho: men's dress, a long-sleeved tunic, worn knee-length and belted at the waist

Gomchen: lay monk or ascetic

Gompa: monastery

Gonkhang: chapel or sanctum of a protecting deity, which women are not allowed to enter

Gup: head of a gewog or county

Guru Padmasambhava: the Indian saint who brought Buddhism to Bhutan in the eighth century; also known as Guru Rimpoche

Hogay: fresh cheese

Jakri: a shaman

Je Khenpo: Chief Abbot of Bhutan, and official head of the Drukpa Kargyupa school; known as the Dharma Raja in British colonial accounts

Je Shacha Rinchen (r. 1744–55): Ninth Chief Abbot of Bhutan, who founded Nobgang village

Jigme Dorji Wangchuck (r. 1952–72): third king of Bhutan

Jigme Namgyel (1825–81): Tongsa Penlop and Fiftieth Desi of Bhutan; father of the first king

Jigme Singye Wangchuck (b. 1955): present king of Bhutan

Jigme Wangchuck (r. 1926–52): second king of Bhutan

Kabney: ceremonial scarf worn by men

Keyra: woven belt for women's kira

Khandoma: celestial maiden, angel; also known as dakini

Khemar: broad red band painted below the eaves, which marks out a building as a religious structure

Kheng: a thickly forested region of central Bhutan, covering the districts of Zhemgang and parts of Mongar

Khenja: jacket worn by the women of Laya

Khuru: a game of darts, with the target placed at a distance of 20 metres

Kira: women's ankle-length dress, made of a piece of woven material the size of a single bed sheet

Koma: a pair of silver brooches, fastening the women's kira at the shoulder

Kunrey: the assembly hall of the monks in a dzong

Kushuthara: an elaborate textile woven in Lhuentse in eastern Bhutan, with multicoloured silks against a white background

La: mountain pass

Lam Neten: head abbot of a district

Lama: Buddhist priest who is a religious master

Langdharma: heretical ninth-century Tibetan king who tried to stamp out Buddhism. He was assassinated by a monk in AD 842.

Layaps: people from Laya in the northern highlands of Bhutan

Lhakhang: Buddhist temple

Lhops: a tribe living in south-western Bhutan, who were among the earliest settlers in the country. Their religion is mainly animist, and their language is called Ngentam.

Lhotsampa: persons of Nepali origin who are settled in Bhutan

Lopon: scholar; also a learned Buddhist theologian

Lozay: a long ballad or a traditional form of debate in verse, in which men are pitted against women

Lunaps: people from Lunana in the northern highlands of Bhutan

Lyonpo: a minister in the Bhutanese government. Lyonpos wear orange scarves.

Mani chukor: prayer wheel driven by water

Mani wall: wall inset with stones carved with the Buddhist mantra *Om mani padme hum* (Hail to the Jewel in the Lotus)

Maru: a dish made with minced dried beef and ginger

Milarepa (1040–1123): revered Tibetan poet and saint

Monpas: an ethnic group in Tongsa district, believed to be the earliest inhabitants of Bhutan. They have their own language, Monkha.

Nepo: host families and trading partners of the Brokpas of Merak and Sakteng, in whose house they stay when they come to the lower valleys in winter

Ney: sacred site

Ngagi Rinchen: Bhutanese name for the fourteenth-century Buddhist saint from India, Vanaratna, who meditated in Bhutan

Ngultrum: Bhutanese currency. One ngultrum is on a par with one Indian rupee.

Nob: jewel

Pagay: traditional Monpa dress, woven of nettle fibre

Palden Lhamo: Mahakali in Sanskrit, female Protecting Deity of Bhutan

Pazaps: Zhabdrung Ngawang Namgyel's warriors

Pema Lingpa (1450–1521): saint and reincarnation of Guru Padmasambhava. The royal family of Bhutan are directly descended from him.

Penlop: historic title given to governors of the three big dzongs of Paro, Tongsa and Daga. The Crown Prince of Bhutan holds the title of Tongsa Penlop.

Phurpa: ritual dagger used during religious ceremonies

Rachu: women's ceremonial scarf, worn draped over the left shoulder

Rimpoche: reincarnate lama

Sendha: ruler in the Bumthang region in the eighth century, also known as Sindhu Raja, who invited Guru Padmasambhava to his kingdom

Senem kurim: religious ritual for purifying the ground

Serda: ceremonial religious procession at the end of the Punakha Domchoe

Sharchopkha: the language spoken in eastern Bhutan

Singcha: a mildly alcoholic drink brewed from wheat

Sokshing: a wooden pole, or 'life tree' interred within a chorten, which symbolically links heaven and earth

Songtsen Gampo: king of Tibet in the seventh century who built the first Buddhist temples in Bhutan

Sowa Rigpa: traditional Bhutanese system of medicine

Suja: salty buttered tea

Takin (*Budorcas taxicolor*): curious-looking national animal of Bhutan, scientifically classified as a goat-antelope; found in the highlands of Bhutan

Tara: female emanation of the Bodhisattva of Compassion

Thangka: religious painting framed in brocade

Tharcham: flag

Thongdrel: large painted or embroidered silk banner hung from the wall of a dzong or monastery on important religious occasions

Torma: ritual religious offering made of rice flour or wheat dough mixed with butter and sculpted into intricate forms

Trulku: reincarnation; spiritual head of a monastery

Tsachhu: hot spring

Tsangpa Gyare Yeshe Dorji (1161–1211): Tibetan saint who founded the Drukpa Kargyupa school of Buddhism

Tsechu: religious festival held in honour of Guru Padmasambhava

Tseringma: Goddess of Long Life and Prosperity

Tshebum: vase containing the water of immortality

Tsho: lake

Tshogdu: National Assembly of Bhutan

Tsipee cham: distinctive black cap with five tail-like projections, worn by the Brokpas of Merak and Sakteng

Tyoko: women's jacket, worn over the kira

Ugyen Wangchuck (r. 1907–26): first king of Bhutan

Utse: central tower of a dzong

Wonju: women's long-sleeved blouse, worn under the kira

Woola: system of compulsory labour tax, in which every community had to contribute their labour for building projects

Yab: father

Yathra: colourful woollen textile woven in the Bumthang district of Bhutan

Yeshe Gompo: Mahakala in Sanskrit, Protecting Deity of Bhutan

Yeti: a giant ape-like creature who is believed to live in the Himalayas but has never been captured, not even on camera. Also known as Abominable Snowman, Bigfoot, or Megay (in eastern Bhutan, where there are many accounts of Yeti-sightings).

Yum: mother

Za: planetary deity

Zaw: toasted rice

Zee: etched agate stone with white lines, a highly prized gem

Zethoey: fermented cheese made in Sakteng

Zhabdrung Jigme Dorji: Sixth Mind Incarnation of Zhabdrung Ngawang Namgyel, who was murdered at Talo in 1931

Zhabdrung Ngawang Namgyel (1594–1651): revered as the founder of the Bhutanese state, he unified Bhutan and established its administrative system.

Zoom: ankle-length skirt worn by the women of Laya

Zorig Chusum: the thirteen classical arts of Bhutan

INDEX